TOP 200 Vegetarian Recipes Cookbook

Written by: Jamie Stewart

Copyright © 2015

All Rights Reserved

All rights reserved. No part of this book may be reproduced or transmitted in any form or by any means, electronic or mechanical, including photocopying, recording or by any information storage and retrieval system, without written permission from the publisher, except for the inclusion of brief quotations in a review.

Warning-Disclaimer

The purpose of this book is to educate and entertain. The author or publisher does not guarantee that anyone following the techniques, suggestions, tips, ideas, or strategies will become successful. The author and publisher shall have neither liability or responsibility to anyone with respect to any loss or damage caused, or alleged to be caused, directly or indirectly by the information contained in this book.

**** Download a FREE PDF file with photos of all the recipes. ****

Table of Contents

TOP 200 Vegetarian Recipes Cookbook	1
PART ONE BREAKFAST	11
Mushroom Sandwich with Mayo and Salad	11
Curry-Veggie Omelet	11
Veggie Baguette Sandwiches	12
(Ready in about 1 hour | Servings 4)	12
Classic Soft Pancakes	13
French Toast with Orange and Vanilla	13
Croustades with Eggs, Peppers and Mushrooms	14
Oatmeal Scones with Cream Cheese	14
Homemade Bread with Cranberries	15
Buns with Homemade Cheese Spread	16
Toasted Bread with Homemade Pesto	16
Delicious Sandwiches with Hummus and Tomatoes	17
Mushrooms and Tomato Frittata	17
Roasted Vegetables and Cheese Frittata	18
Sunday Vegetable-Tofu Frittata	18
Vegetable and Swiss Cheese Omelet	19
Apricot and Almonds Granola	20
Scrambled Cheese with Tomatoes	20
Fruit Bread With Sour Cream	21
Quick Grits with Ginger	21
Baked Grits with Eggs and Tomatoes	22
Hot Veggie and Mozzarella Sandwiches	22
Chilli Cheese Omelet	23
Baked Avocado with Grapefruit and Endive	23
Quesadillas with Hummus and Spinach	24
Edamame-Cashwes Pâté Sandwiches	24
Easy Honey Cornbread	25
Crunchy Spiced Sandwiches	25
Refreshing Quinoa Salad	26
Fruity Family Breakfast	27

Honey Lentil Loaves	27
Quick Tropical Oatmeal	28
Figs Carrot Loaf	28
Toasted Bread with Homemade Prune Spread	29
Berry Oatmeal with Almonds	29
Homemade Cinnamon Rolls	30
Healthy Grain Fruit Breakfast	30
Pita Bread with Tzatziki and Boiled Eggs	31
English Muffins with Tempeh and Sauce	32
Crispy-Soft Filo Triangles	33
Classic French Toast	33
PART TWO LUNCH	**34**
Zucchini Soup with Baby Spinach	34
Cauliflower-Cheese Soup	34
Chickpea Stew with Couscous	35
Mexican Chili-Enchilada Stew	36
Spiced Vegetables and Rice with Cashews	36
Lentil-Chickpea Stew with Currants	37
Thick Bean and Potato Soup	38
Tahini and Chickpea Broth	38
Quick Cheese Soup	39
Vegetarian-style 'Bolognese'	40
Spanish Vegetable Paella	41
Spinach Cannelloni with Béchamel	41
Creamed Mushroom Tagliatelle	42
Creamy Spiced Tomatoes	43
Chilled Summer Soup	43
Broccoli Rabe with Cheese	44
Two-Bean Chili with Cheese	44
Baked Asparagus in Sauce	45
Buttery Carrots with Basmati Rice	45
Summer Stuffed Tomatoes with Pesto	46
Rice Zucchini-Tomato Casserole	46
Chilled Picnic Soup	47
Baked Spiced Zucchini and Potatoes	47

Chilled Yogurt Cucumber Soup with Almonds	48
Iced Cucumber and Watercress Soup	48
Mushrooms Pasta Casserole	49
Mom's Creamy Cheesy Cabbage	49
Creamy Yam Soup	50
Exotic Curried Stew with Coconut Milk	51
Greens and Potatoes Casserole	52
Chickpea and Ginger Stew with Yogurt	52
Quick Asparagus Frittata	53
Chickpeas in Cream Sauce	53
Vegetables with Cheese and Pumpkin Seeds	54
Quick Fried Spiced Corn	54
Stuffed Tomatoes with Cheese and Almonds	55
Potato and Onion Broth	55
Veggie BBQ with Soy Marinade	56
Fava Beans with Herbs and Tomatoes	56
Greens with Herbs and Yogurt	57
Garlicky Jerusalem Artichokes in Wine Sauce	58
Kohlrabi with Horseradish and Sour Cream	58
Baked Mushrooms with Almonds	59
Pasta with Caramelized Scallions and Walnuts	59
Curried Parsnips with Chutney	60
Stir-Fried Peas and Carrots with Sichuan Pepper Salt	60
Italian Juicy Peperonata	61
Three-Peppers Tomato Stew	61
PART THREE DINNER	**62**
Fresh Vegetable Spring Rolls	62
Crunchy Pea Bites	63
Vegetarian Sausages with Vegetables	63
Easy Seitan Burgers	64
Spicy Salad with Peanut Dressing and Croutons	64
Rutabaga and Carrot Gratin	65
Stir-Fried Asparagus with Tofu and Chestnuts	66
Braised Tofu and Veggies in Sauce	66
Mango and Avocado Light Salad	67

Lentil and Broccoli Salad with Chilli and Coriander	68
Pita Bread with Greek Salad	68
Quick French Bread Pizza	69
Indian Vegetable Bondas	69
Chilli-Coriander Rice	70
Italian Tomato-Rosemary Bruschetta	71
Italian-style Pasta Salad	71
Avocado Salad Bowl with Corn Chips	72
Bucatini and Asparagus with Sauce	72
Quick Vegetable Tagine	73
Crustless Cauliflower-Cheese Pie	74
Buttermilk Onion Tart	74
Eggplant and Tomato Tart with Herbs	75
Cornmeal Bean and Tomato Pie	76
Vegetable and Cheese Burritos	76
Spiced Vegetable Patties	77
Mediterranean Ratatouille	78
Mexican Chalupas	78
Avocado Sandwiches with Eggs	79
Bean and Cheese Tostadas	79
Noodles and Cauliflower Stir-Fry	80
Mushroom Cheeseburgers	80
Curry Vegetables with Tofu and Coconut	81
Macaroni Like Grandma Used to Make	81
Hot Tomato and Cheese Sandwiches	82
Breaded Cheese Ravioli	82
Potato Salad with Spinach	83
Bean Tostadas with Greens and Salsa	83
Curried Tempeh Tacos	84
Spiced Vegetable Pizza	85
Smoked Cheese and Zucchini Pizza	85
PART FOUR FAST SNACKS	**86**
Quick Guacamole with Sour Cream	86
Carrot and Zucchini Wraps	86
Chickpea Chili Bites	87

Toasted Rye Bread with Creamy Mushrooms	88
Garlicky and Creamy Stuffed Mushrooms	88
Garlic-Parmesan Bread with Tomato Dip	89
Homemade Tortilla Chips with Salsa	89
Lentil Spread with Slipper Bread	90
Mini Pita with Greek Dip	90
Mini Pita Pockets with Spiced Eggs	91
Cheese Herb Spread with Crackers	91
Ricotta Spread with Pepper Strips	92
Brussels Sprout Chips with Cheese	92
Pita Bread Triangles with Eggplant Dip	93
Stuffed Mushrooms with Feta and Herbs	93
Spiced Corn Crackers	94
Apple Pecan Popcorn	95
Baked Mushrooms with Cheese and Eggs	95
Pecan Popcorn with Delicious Syrup	96
Red Quinoa and Avocado Appetizer	96
Stuffed Peppadews Bites	97
Party Potato Cakes	97
Garbanzo Bean-Cumin Dip with Corn Crackers	98
Tarator Sauce with Fried Vegetables	98
Party Baby Reubens	99
Pecans and Cashews Snack Mix	99
Cheese Mini Bruschetta	100
Fig-Almonds and Cheese Canapés	100
Mini Fruit and Cinnamon Triangles	101
Honey-Roasted Peanuts Spread	101
Tortilla Chips with Hot Spinach Dip	102
Garlicky Breadsticks with Tomato Sauce	102
Teatime Parmesan Popovers	103
Basic Glazed Onions	103
Stuffed Okra Fingers	104
Spiced Cheese Poppers	104
Stuffed Celery Fingers	105
Bruschetta with Eggplant and Feta	105

Party Spiced Stuffed Eggs	106
PART FIVE DESSERTS	**107**
Almond Summertime Treat	107
Fruit-Nuts Ice Cream	107
Chocolate Maraschino Cakes	108
Cream Pudding Cake	108
Grandma's Chocolate Pie	109
Chocolate Sauce with Fresh Fruit	109
Caramels for Party Gifts	110
Chocolate Cinnamon Loaf	110
Chocolate Squares with Nuts and Coconut	111
Carrot Cake with Almonds and Cheese Icing	112
Pears with Chocolate Sauce	112
Perfect Cake for the Evening	113
Halloween Pumpkin Cheesecake	113
Creamy Dessert in a Glass	114
Perfect Blackberry Ice Cream	114
Pecan Vanilla Ice Cream	115
Mom's Butter Cake	115
The Best Gingerbread Ever	116
Peach and Almond Cake	117
Holiday Fruit Tart	117
Apple Crisp with Ice Cream	118
Stuffed Peaches on Almond-Flavored Whipped Cream	119
Peanut Butter Oatmeal Cookies	119
Pears with Almond Topping	120
Frozen Honey and Pistachios Mousse	120
Chocolate Avocado Mousse	122
Cardamom Butter Cookies	122
Teatime Sandwich Cookies	123
Peanut Butter Cookies	124
Download a FREE PDF file with photos of all the recipes by following the link:	124

Why Vegetarian?

Food is an important part of our lives, but not only in terms of nutrition. Eating ought to make us feel good physically as well as mentally. There are many diet, but vegetarian diet is so unique that it requires special attention and clarification.

Who this book is intended for?

Good food attracts loved ones and close friends together. It doesn't matter if you are having a quick noon meal with your good friend, an enjoyable pack lunch with a colleague or romantic dinner with a wife or husband – these events play an integral part in our everyday lives.

Because you are reading this book, you undoubtedly have some affinity for learning more facts about the vegetarian diet and lifestyle, or you're a vegetarian, already. You could possibly just want to lower your consumption of meat. It could be that your friend or member of the family has decided to become a vegetarian, therefore you want to show your full support. Actually, there are many good reasons to have and use this cookbook.

If you have recently chosen a vegetarian lifestyle, this cookbook is the right place to start. You can get a lot of inspiring ideas and you will understand the beauty of vegetarian cuisine. On the other hand, if you are experienced vegetarian, you will also find a lot of tips and hints to improve the quality of your diet. This cookbook is created to suit the delicate personal preference of the longtime vegetarians, as well as the newbies who are looking for products and solutions that they should consider.

Vegetarian diet is an integral part of the culture of many nations. In modern times, people usually choose a vegetarian diet for personal ethical reasons. Vegetarians often say: "I don't eat anything with a face on it". Some people are concerned about the fact that we are going to run out of food. Of course, there are some religious orientations, so people just follow the rules and beliefs. There are people who choose vegetarianism for health reasons because they are fight obesity, diabetes, heart disease and so on. If you want to influence your children to eat more fruits and vegetables, these fun and creative recipes can help you. Regardless of the reason, vegetarianism is not only a new approach to food but also a new approach to life!

How this cookbook can come in handy?

There is absolutely no doubt, that those who choose to go vegetarian for better health, can expect an improvement in the overall psycho-physical health. But, things are not so simple. Vegetarians have to be pretty sure that their bodies are getting all the necessary nutritional substances. Nevertheless, only the rejection of meat from the diet does not automatically mean good effects on our health. We constantly read and listen to information about the harmful effects of meat on human health. Cholesterol, saturated fat and animal hormones from animal meat are the real enemies of human health, and we all know that. On the other hand, meat is an important source of protein, which is necessary for the optimal function of our body. Each time you plan daily meals for you and your family, you can also make pretty sure that you include all important foods from each food group. Your meals should be well balanced. You have to learn about new sources of protein for you such as soybean products, tofu, chickpeas, oats, avocado, beets, brown rice and so on. Once you understand the beauty and quality of vegetarian food, nothing will ever be the same again. You will be healthy, happy and full of energy!

Then, proteins are very important, but we should not forget about the other nutrients. There is a certain amount of vitamins and minerals that we must take on a daily basis, regardless of the diet. For example, how to compensate for the lack of calcium? Very good sources of calcium are whole grains, nuts, and legumes, broccoli, kale etc. Then, you need to know how much fluids you need to drink during the day. Of course, you have to pay special attention to the fat and carbohydrates. Eating specific combinations of foods in your vegetarian meal, you supply your body with complete nutrients. Sure, you do not have to think of your meals because this book will come in handy in the kitchen. These recipes are adjusted to meet the daily nutritional needs of the human body.

Of course, this is not rigid guide, feel free to try new combinations. These are guidelines and suggestions which you should follow in order to be safe and healthy. For example, if you want to lose weight, you can reduce the fat content of represented dishes. You can lower amount of the oil or butter you use, or you can use low-fat cooking spray. You can also use a skim milk instead of whole milk. Then, you can try to use a different combination of spices. As you can see, you have many options to customize this cookbook according to your need and taste. So, the options are endless, let your imagination run wild!

Now we are cooking!

Our cookbook contains proven and verified recipes, which provide you with the best pleasure in meals. Recipes are classified into five categories: breakfast, lunch, dinner, fast snacks and desserts. Altogether, the book contains 200 vegetarian recipes for any occasion and for every taste! Whether you're a vegetarian or a meat eater, you will enjoy exploring and discovering new foods.

When we mention any vegetarian cuisine, people think of vegetables and fruits, first of all. However, when people find out that vegetarian cuisine is more than interesting, vivid and very healthy, they will often look for the vegetarian recipes. Certainly, if you're still not sure of your decision to become a vegetarian, go check it out. Try, explore, have fun! You have nothing to lose! This book can help you to make your final decision, who knows?

You do not have to be vegetarian in order to enjoy these amazing meals! This cookbook is a good companion to keep handy. You will find inspiration for everyday meals, as well as for the preparation of festive meals. This cookbook can help you in the several ways:

You get complete information for the preparation of each dish, including Ingredients, Directions, Preparation time and Serving size.

You get a well-balanced and nutritionally very valuable meals that are easy to prepare. In this way, you can always plan your time and your budget. It's easy: Write down the foods from the list of the ingredients and go to the grocery store. Utterly relaxing, right?

These various mouth-watering recipes from all over the world offer you a wide variety of the flavors and aromas. You will always be able to prepare new dishes or old dishes in different ways. This means you will no longer have any trouble with boring vegetarian diet.

"It is my view that the vegetarian manner of living, by its purely physical effect on the human temperament, would most beneficially influence the lot of mankind." Albert Einstein said.

Some people said the cooking is taking up all their spare time. You will see that it does not have to be like that by using this cookbook. This cookbook contains proven good and highly imaginative recipes that everyone can prepare and everyone could eat. It only takes a little time and a little more love and desire. There are a lot of good reasons to cook your vegetarian recipes at home. Here are just a few of them:

You control the ingredients that you use. If you purchase a vegetarian meal at a fast food that does not necessarily mean it is healthy eating. For example, French fries or fried foods.

You save money.

Healthy and happy family. You can make happy your family with very healthy meals. That is a priceless feeling!

Planning and keep it simple. Organizing ahead of time will help you make much better meal choices. On the other hand, you save your time and energy.

Cooking can be a joyful experience. It is a passion and satisfaction that cannot be compared with anything in the world!

Be inspired! Make these great meatless dishes and treat your family and guests. We give you these recipes with great love in the hope it will inspire you and it will make you happy.

PART ONE BREAKFAST

Mushroom Sandwich with Mayo and Salad

(Ready in about 20 minutes | Servings 4)

Ingredients

5 large mushrooms, sliced

2 tablespoons canola oil

2 medium tomatoes, sliced

1 teaspoon salt

Freshly ground black pepper to taste

8 butter lettuce leaves

1 tablespoon olive oil

1 teaspoon Dijon Mustard

2 tablespoons Mayonnaise

4 large whole grain ciabatta rolls

Directions

Heat the oil in a large saucepan over medium heat. Cook the sliced mushrooms until cooked through and soft, for about 10 minutes.

To make your sandwiches: Cut each ciabatta roll in halves. On a half of each roll, place the mushrooms, and then place the sliced tomato. Add salt and freshly ground black pepper.

Layer lettuce leaves and drizzle some olive oil. Adjust the seasonings and add mustard and mayonnaise. Garnish with lettuce leaves and serve immediately.

Curry-Veggie Omelet

(Ready in about 30 minutes | Servings 2)

Ingredients

1 medium tomato, peeled

1 boiled potato, diced

4 eggs

2 tablespoons canola oil

1 onion, chopped

2 cloves garlic, minced

1 teaspoon turmeric powder

1 teaspoon chilli powder

1 teaspoon salt

1 teaspoon freshly ground black pepper

1 teaspoon dried rosemary

Directions

Prepare boiled potato. Mash a tomato with a masher or a fork until smooth.

Heat the oil in a medium saucepan. Sauté the onions and garlic with mashed tomato for 5 minutes till the onions are tender.

Beat the eggs and combine with potato, turmeric powder and chilli powder. Reduce the heat to medium-low temperature.

Season with salt and freshly ground black pepper add a cup of lukewarm water and cook for 25 minutes.

Garnish with rosemary and serve warm.

Veggie Baguette Sandwiches
(Ready in about 1 hour | Servings 4)

Ingredients

1 large Eggplant	1 large onion, finely chopped
1 red pepper pepper, seeded	1/2 teaspoon salt
1 yellow pepper, seeded	1/4 teaspoon freshly ground black pepper
2 zucchini, sliced lengthways	1 teaspoon spices for tzatziki
5 cloves garlic	2 medium tomatoes, sliced
4 tablespoon extra-virgin olive oil	1 long French baguette

Directions

Preheat the oven to 425 degrees F. Prepare a baking pan.

Slice the eggplant lengthwise into thin slices and salt them generously. Plase in a colander and set aside for 30 minutes. After that, drain and rinse the eggplant slices under cold water.

Place the eggplant, peppers and zucchini slices in a single layer in the baking pan, and add garlic cloves. Season with salt, black pepper and tzatziki. Then pour over 3 tablespoons olive oil. Roast for 20 minutes, or until the garlic is tender.

Meanwhile, heat the remaining tablespoon of oil in a saucepan and sauté the onion until tender and translucent.

Cut the baguette lengthwise. Add the garlic cloves onto the baguette. Place the onion and vegetables along the length of the bread. Top with tomato slices. Adjust the seasonings.

Cut the prepared baguette into four equal pieces.

Classic Soft Pancakes

(Ready in about 1 hour | Servings 4)

Ingredients

2½ cups whole wheat pastry flour

1 tablespoon baking powder

1 teaspoon salt

1 teaspoon brown sugar

2 eggs, beaten

2 cups milk

2 tablespoons pure maple syrup

6 tablespoons butter, melted

Non-stick cooking spray

Maple syrup or heavy whipping cream

Directions

Sift the flour in a large bowl, and add baking powder, salt and sugar.

Beat the eggs with the milk and maple syrup until the mixture is well mixed. To make a batter: Combine wet mixture with the dry ingredients and melted butter and mix until all ingredients are blended. Let stand for 15 minutes.

Heat a frying pan over high-medium heat and add a non-stick spray to coat the bottom. To fry pancakes, spoon some batter into the pan. Carefully, flip pancake over once the surface is covered with golden brown bubbles. Repeat with the remaining pancakes.

Serve with maple syrup or heavy whipping cream and serve immediately.

French Toast with Orange and Vanilla

(Ready in about 40 minutes | Servings 8)

Ingredients

5 eggs

1/3 cup milk

1/3 cup sugar

2 tablespoons orange juice

1 tablespoon orange zest

1½ teaspoons vanilla extract

16 slices slightly stale French bread, sliced diagonally

2 tablespoons butter

confectioners' sugar (optional)

Directions

Beat the eggs thoroughly in a large bowl. Add the milk, sugar, orange juice, orange zest, and vanilla extract and mix all ingredients well.

Add the slices of bread into prepared mixture and let it soak, turning occasionally. It takes about 15 minutes.

Heat the butter in a wide havy skillet over medium heat. Fry French toast on each side until golden brown. Dust with confectioners' sugar and serve warm.

Croustades with Eggs, Peppers and Mushrooms

(Ready in about 30 minutes | Servings 4)

Ingredients

4 slices loaf bread of choice

4 tablespoons butter, melted

1 red green pepper, seeded and chopped

1 yellow bell pepper, seeded and chopped

4-5 button mushrooms, finely sliced

8 eggs

1/4 cup milk

1/4 teaspoon dried basil

1 teaspoon fine sea salt

Freshly ground pepper to taste

Red pepper flakes to taste

Parsley for garnish

Directions

Preheat the oven to 300 degrees F. Prepare a baking sheet.

Cut the crusts from the bread slices. Tear out the center of each slice, leaving a 3/4-inch wall. Brush the bread slices with 2 tablespoons of melted butter.

To make Croustades: Place bread slices on prepared baking sheet and bake for 5 minutes.

Heat 2 tablespoon of the butter in a wide saucepan over medium heat. Cook the peppers and mushrooms until they are soft.

Beat the eggs with milk, basil, salt, black pepper and red pepper flakes. Add the egg mixture in a saucepan, stirring frequently. Make sure not to overcook eggs.

Transfer the croustades on serving plates and spoon equal amounts of eggs into the center of each croustade. Garnish with parsley and serve immediately.

Oatmeal Scones with Cream Cheese

(Ready in about 45 minutes | Servings 8)

Ingredients

1 cup rolled oats

1/2 cup low-fat yogurt

1 cup whole wheat flour

2 tablespoons brown sugar

1 teaspoons baking powder

1 teaspoon baking soda

1/2 teaspoon salt

4 tablespoons butter

2 eggs

1 teaspoon cumin

cream cheese of choice, for garnish

Directions

Preheat the oven to 400 degrees F. Line a baking sheet with parchment paper.

Mix the oats and yogurt in a mixing bowl and let it soak for 15 minutes.

In another bowl sift the flour, then add sugar, baking powder, baking soda, and salt and mix until well combined. Cut the butter into the mixture with a pastry blender.

Beat 1 egg and add to the oatmeal mixture. Stir in the flour mixture, mix and then gather into a ball.

Transfer the mixture onto a floured suface and knead several times. Shape into a circle and cut the circle into 8 equal pieces. Place the dough on the baking sheet.

Beat the remaining egg, and brush each scone. Sprinkle cumin seeds and bake for 16 minutes, or until the scones are golden. Spread the cheese over warm scones and serve immediately.

Homemade Bread with Cranberries

(Ready in about 1 hour 15 minutes | Servings 8)

Ingredients

2 ½ cups pastry flour

1/2 cup whole wheat flour

1/2 cup sugar

1 teaspoon salt

2 teaspoons baking soda

4 tablespoons butter, cut into bits

1 cup cranberries

2 tablespoons sesame seeds

1 ½ cups plain low-fat yogurt

Milk to brush on top

Directions

Preheat the oven to 350 degrees F. Butter a baking pan.

Mix the flours, sugar, salt, and baking soda in a large mixing bowl and stir well to combine.

Add the cut-up butter. Knead the mixture until it resembles coarse meal. Add the cranberries and sesame seeds and mix well.

Add yogurt and stir until the dough is wetted.

Transfer the dough onto floured surface and knead several times, until it is sticky. Form the dough to your baking pan.

Put the dough in the prepared baking pan. Brush the top of the dough with a little bit of milk.

Bake your bread for 60 minutes, or until golden brown. Then let cool thoroughly on a wire rack.

Buns with Homemade Cheese Spread

(Ready in about 15 minutes + 2 hours chilling | Servings 6)

Ingredients

2 cups plain low-fat yogurt

1 clove garlic, minced

1 tablespoon extra-virgin olive oil

1 teaspoon dried rosemary

1 tablespoon fresh basil, minced

1 teaspoon fresh oregano

1/2 teaspoon freshly ground black pepper

6 buns of choice

Directions

Line a strainer with cheesecloth. Put the strainer over a large bowl. Pour the yogurt into the center of the strainer and place in the fridge. Let stand overnight.

Cheese should have the consistency of ricotta cheese. Transfer the homemade cheese in a small bowl.

Mix garlic, olive oil, rosemary, basil, oregano, and pepper. Chill for 2 hours before serving. Serve with your favorite buns.

Toasted Bread with Homemade Pesto

(Ready in about 20 minutes | Servings 6)

Ingredients

3 bunches fresh basil leaves

1/2 cup olive oil

1/3 cup pine nuts

2 garlic cloves

1/4 cup Parmesan cheese, grated

1/4 cup pecorino Sardo, freshly grated

1 teaspoon fine sea salt

freshly ground black pepper to taste

12 bread slices

Directions

Mix basil leaves, oil, pine nuts and garlic in an electric blender or a food processor.

Process until the mixture has a paste form. Add Parmesan, Pecorino Sardo, salt and pepper and process until smooth. Place the pesto in a small bowl.

Meanwhile, bake the bread slices in a toaster oven broiler.

Spread 1 tablespoon of pesto on each slice of toasted bread, garnish with basile leaves and serve.

Delicious Sandwiches with Hummus and Tomatoes

(Ready in about 1 hour | Servings 6)

Ingredients

16-ounce can chickpeas

3 cloves garlic, minced

fresh juice from 2 large lemons

3/4 cup tahini

1/2 teaspoon salt

1/4 teaspon freshly ground black pepper

1/2 teaspon red pepper flakes

1/2 cup cold water

1 tablespoon extra-virgin olive oil

3 medium tomatoes, sliced

12 Bread slices

Directions

Rinse and drain the chickpeas.

Combine the chickpeas, garlic, lemon juice, tahini, salt, black pepper and red pepper in a food processor. Then pour in the water and add olive oil.

If the hummus is too thick, add a little more water and blend again.

Replace into a medium bowl, cover, and chill before serving. To make sandwiches: Spread the chilled hummus over bread slices and layer tomato slices. Adjust the seasonings and serve.

Mushrooms and Tomato Frittata

(Ready in about 1 hour | Servings 4)

Ingredients

8 eggs

1/4 cup milk

1/4 cup Parmesan cheese, grated

1/2 teaspoon salt

1/4 teaspoon freshly ground black pepper

1/4 teaspoon smoked paprika

3 tablespoons olive oil

2 yellow onions, finely chopped

28-ounce can tomatoes, diced

1 teaspoon dried rosemary

5-6 button mushrooms

non-stick cooking spray

Directions

Preheat the oven to 325 degrees F. Oil a pie plate with non-stick spray.

Beat together the eggs, milk, Parmesan cheese, salt, pepper and paprika.

Heat the oil in a wide heavy skillet over medium-high heat. Sauté the onions until they are translucent.

Add drained and diced tomatoes and rosemary, and cook for 8 minutes longer, stirring constantly.

Add the mushrooms and cook until tender. Add vegetable mixture to the eggs and mix to combine all ingredients. Place into the pie plate.

Bake the frittata until a toothpick inserted into the center of the frittata comes clean, or for 17 minutes. Cut into 4 pieces, garnish with tomatoes and serve warm.

Roasted Vegetables and Cheese Frittata

(Ready in about 1 hour | Servings 4)

Ingredients

2 potatoes, peeled and diced

3 yellow onions, chopped

2 tablespoon olive oil

1/2 teaspoon salt

1/4 freshly ground black pepper

1/2 teaspoon dried basil

8 eggs

1/2 cup Gouda, grated

1 clove garlic, minced

10 Olives of choice pitted

Fresh parsley (optional)

Directions

Preheat the oven to 400 degrees F. Line a large baking sheet with parchment paper. Butter a pie plate and set aside.

Combine the potatoes, onions and olive oil and spread onto the baking sheet in one single layer. Bake for 30 minutes. Toss after the first 15 minutes.

Remove from the oven and season with salt, pepper, and basil. Reserve.

In the meantime, reduce the oven heat to 325 degrees F.

Beat the eggs in a medium bowl and add the cooled potato mixture. Then add grated cheese and garlic. Pour the mixture into the prepared pie plate.

Bake 25 to 30 minutes, garnish with olives and parsley and serve warm.

Sunday Vegetable-Tofu Frittata

(Ready in about 4 hours 30 minutes | Servings 4)

Ingredients

2 tablespoons canola oil

1 small onion, chopped

1 cup potatoes, peeled and diced

2 red peppers, diced

1 teaspoon jalapeño, minced

1 clove garlic, minced

2 tablespoon parsley

16 ounces firm tofu, crumbled

1/2 cup milk

4 teaspoons cornstarch

1 teaspoon mustard

1 teaspoon salt

1/4 teaspoon black pepper

1/4 teaspoon red pepper flakes

Directions

Heat the oil in a slow cooker. Sauté the onions, potatoes, peppers, jalapeño, and garlic over low-medium heat for 20 minutes.

Process parsley, tofu, milk, cornstarch, mustard and spices in a food processor until smooth.

Pour the mixture into the slow cooker with the vegetables.

Cover and cook frittata on medium-high heat for 4 hours.

Vegetable and Swiss Cheese Omelet

(Ready in about 30 minutes | Servings 2)

Ingredients

2 scallions, chopped

3 tablespoons butter

1 green bell pepper, chopped

4 eggs

2 tablespoons milk

1/2 teaspoon salt

1/4 teaspoon freshly ground black pepper

1 teaspoon dried basil

1/4 cup Swiss cheese, shredded

Parsley for garnish

Directions

Melt 2 tablespoons butter in a wide saucepan over high-medium heat. Sauté the scallions and bell pepper for 5 minutes, or until the scallions are tender.

Beat the eggs with the milk, and season with salt and pepper.

Melt the remaining 1 tablespoon butter in the saucepan over medium heat. When the butter is bubbly, add the egg mixture and cook for 5 minutes, until the center of the eggs begins to look dry.

Place the shredded cheese over the omelet and spoon the vegetables into the center of the prepared omelet. Fold one edge of the omelet over the vegetables.

Cook for two minutes more, until the cheese melts. Divide the omelet among two serving plates, sprinkle parsley and serve warm.

Apricot and Almonds Granola

(Ready in about 1 hour 30 minutes | Servings 6)

Ingredients

2 cups rolled oats

1/2 cup spelt flour

1/2 cup sugar

1 teaspoon ground cinnamon

3 tablespoons olive oil

1/4 cup applesauce

3 tablespoons maple syrup

1/4 cup dried apricots, diced

1/4 cup almonds, chopped

2 tablespoons flax seeds, ground

2 tablespoons sesame seeds

Directions

Preheat oven to 300 degrees F.

Line a cookie sheet with parchment paper.

To make granola: Combine the rolled oats, spelt flour, sugar, cinnamon, oil, applesauce, maple syrup, apricots, almonds, ground flax seeds and sesame seeds in a large bowl, and stir to mix well all ingredients.

Spread the granola on the prepared cookie sheet.

Bake for 35 minutes until the granola is completely dry. Serve chilled.

Scrambled Cheese with Tomatoes

(Ready in about 30 minutes | Servings 4)

Ingredients

1 tablespoon olive oil

1 bunch scallions, chopped

1 (14.5 ounce) can tomatoes, diced

1 (12 ounce) package firm silken tofu, drained and crumbled

1/2 teaspoon fine sea salt

1/4 teaspoon black pepper

1/4 teaspoon smoked paprika

1/2 cup shredded hard cheese of choice

Directions

Heat olive oil in an iron-skillet over medium-high heat. Sauté the scallions until they are tender.

Stir in tomatoes together with their juice and firm silken tofu.

Season with salt, pepper, and smoked paprika. Continue cooking until heated through, for about 10 minutes.

Sprinkle the cheese and serve immediately.

Fruit Bread With Sour Cream

(Ready in about 1 hour 20 minutes | Servings 10)

Ingredients

1 ¾ cups pastry flour

1 teaspoon baking powder

1/2 teaspoon salt

1/4 teaspoon cinnamon

1/2 cup butter, melted

3/4 cup brown sugar

2 eggs

1/2 cup sour cream

1 teaspoon vanilla

1 cups fresh strawberries

1/4 cups fresh blueberries

3/4 cup hazelnuts

confectioners' sugar for garnish

Directions

Preheat the oven to 350 degrees F. Butter a loaf pan and set aside.

Mix the flour, baking powder, salt, and cinnamon. Reserve.

Beat butter until smooth. Gradually add sugar and continue to beat. Add brown sugar. Then stir in eggs, one at a time. Stir in sour cream and vanilla, and mix well to combine all ingredients.

Add strawberries, blueberries and hazelnuts.

Pour the dough into the loaf pan. Bake for 60 to 65 minutes. Let stand on a rack to cool. Dust with confectioners' sugar if desired and serve with hot milk.

Quick Grits with Ginger

(Ready in about 35 minutes | Servings 4)

Ingredients

2 cups water

1 ¼ cups milk

1/2 teaspoon salt

1 cup quick cooking grits

1 tablespoon grated ginger

1/4 cup butter

Directions

Bring a stockpot of water, milk, and salt to a boil. Gradually add grits into boiling mixture. Then add grated ginger.

Stir frequently until hominy is well mixed.

Cover stockpot, reduce the heat to law and simmer for 30 minutes, stirring often.

Grits should have a consistency of stiff cream of wheat. Then add the butter.

Serve hot with butter or cheese.

Baked Grits with Eggs and Tomatoes

(Ready in about 30 minutes | Servings 4)

Ingredients

1 onion, finely chopped

2 cloves garlic, minced

2 medium tomatoes, finely chopped

1 teaspoon salt

1/4 teaspoon freshly ground black pepper

2 cups water

1 cup quick cooking grits

1 tablespoon butter

4 eggs

Directions

Preheat the oven to 425 degrees F. Butter a baking dish.

Heat a butter in a wide saucepan and sauté the onions and garlic for about 5 minutes. Add tomatoes and cook for 15 minutes more. Season with salt and pepper.

Bring water to a boil and add quick cooking grits. Cover and simmer, stirring occasionally, until grits are cooked, or 5 minutes.

Make a few wells in the top of the cooked grits and pour tomato mixture into wells. Add whole eggs over tomato mixture, adjust the seasonings and bake. Bake your meal until the whites of the eggs have set, for about 15 minutes.

Hot Veggie and Mozzarella Sandwiches

(Ready in about 50 minutes | Servings 5)

Ingredients

3 medium zucchini, sliced lengthwise

1 large eggplant, sliced lengthwise

1 teaspoon salt

1/2 teaspoon black pepper

1/2 teaspoon smoked paprika

1/4 cup olive oil

1 ¾ cups mozzarella, grated

3/4 cup pesto

1 French baguette

Directions

Preheat the oven to 325 degrees F. Prepare a baking dish.

Season the zucchini and eggplant slices with salt, black pepper and smoked paprika. Place the vegetables in a bowl and pour in the olive oil.

Bake the zucchini and eggplant until cooked through.

Cut the baguette lengthwise into 5 equal portions. Spread the pesto sauce over bread.

Place the vegetables and top with Mozzarella cheese.

Wrap each sandwich with aluminum foil.

Bake sandwiches for 30 minutes.

Chilli Cheese Omelet

(Ready in about 20 minutes | Servings 2)

Ingredients

1 tablespoon olive oil

2 scallions, sliced

3 large eggs, beaten

1 teaspoon chilli powder

1 green chilli, finely chopped

1 teaspoon chili powder

1 teaspoon fine sea salt

1/2 black pepper

semi-soft cheese, 4 strips

coriander leaves for garnish

Directions

Heat olive oil in a wide saucepan. The oil must be heated to the right temperature and then add the scallions. Sauté the scallions for 5 to 6 minutes.

Beat the eggs in a bowl and pour in saucepan. Then add green chili and chili powder. Season with salt and pepper. Cook for 5 minutes and add the cheese strips. Cover and cook for another 7 to 8 minutes.

Garnish with coriander leaves and serve immediately.

Baked Avocado with Grapefruit and Endive

(Ready in about 25 minutes | Servings 4)

Ingredients

2 tablespoon olive oil

2 cups endives, halved and sliced crosswise into half-moons

2 shallots, sliced

2 tablespoons parsley, chopped

1 teaspoon fine sea salt

1/4 teaspoon freshly ground black pepper

2 avocados, pitted

1 grapefruit, peeled and sliced

Juice of one fresh lemon

Coriander leaves for garnish

Directions

Preheat oven to 425 degrees F. Prepare a non-stick baking dish.

Heat oil in a heavy skillet over medium-high heat. Sauté the shallots and endives until the shallots are tender and translucent.

Stir in parsley, and add salt and pepper.

Cut the avocados into halves and place in the baking dish. Add prepared endive mixture.

Bake for 13 minutes, till the vegetables begin to brown.

Drizzle lemon juice, garnish with grapefruit slices and coriander leaves. Serve immediately.

Quesadillas with Hummus and Spinach

(Ready in about 20 minutes | Servings 4)

Ingredients

1/4 cup cilantro leaves

1 clove garlic, peeled

3/4 cup cooked chickpeas rinsed and drained

1 tablespoon lemon juice

1 tablespoon lemon zest

2 tablespoon extra-virgin olive oil

2 tablespoon water

2 (7-inch) whole-wheat pitas, split crosswise

2 canned red bell peppers, drained and sliced

3/4 cup spinach leaves

Directions

Preheat oven to 350 degrees F. Prepare a baking tray.

To prepare Hummus: Process cilantro and garlic in a blender until finely chopped.

Drain and rinse chickpeas. Add chickpeas, lemon juice, lemon zest, oil, water and blend until the mixture is creamy.

To prepare Quesadillas: Place 2 pita halves on the baking tray. Spread with prepared Hummus.

Add peppers and spinach, and top with remaining pita halves. Bake about 10 minutes.

Cut into desired triangles, sprinkle with additional cilantro leaves and serve immediately.

Edamame-Cashwes Pâté Sandwiches

(Ready in about 15 minutes | Servings 4)

Ingredients

8 slices bread of choice

1¼ cups edamame, shelled

1/2 cup cashwes

1/3 cup mint leaves

1 onion, chopped

1 teaspoon salt

1/4 teaspoon freshly ground black pepper

2 tablespoons lemon zest

3 tablespoons water

2 cups arugula

4 jarred roasted red peppers, drained

2 small tomatoes, thinly sliced

Directions

To prepare edamame pâté: Purée edamame, cashwes, mint leaves, onion, salt and black pepper in a blender until the mixture is finely chopped.

Add lemon zest and water and blend until smooth.

Spoon pâté (aproximatelly 5 tablespoons) and spread over 1 bread slice.

Add 1/2 cup arugula, 1 roasted pepper, and layer tomato slices. Repeat procedure with the other 3 bread slices.

Top with remaining bread slices and serve immediately.

Easy Honey Cornbread

(Ready in about 25 minutes | Servings 6)

Ingredients

Butter to grease a pan

1 cup yellow cornmeal

1 cup whole wheat flour

1 teaspoon baking powder

1/8 cup olive oil

2 tablespoons honey

1 cup milk

Directions

Preheat oven to 425 degrees F. Butter a baking pan and set aside.

Mix together flours and add baking powder. Then add olive oil, honey and milk. Mix well to combine all ingredients.

Bake approximately 15 minutes or until a toothpick or a fork inserted in the center of the loaf comes out clean.

Serve warm with butter and honey.

Crunchy Spiced Sandwiches

(Ready in about 15 minutes | Servings 4)

Ingredients

whole-wheat French bread, sliced into 8 pieces

2 tablespoons Dijon mustard

3 oz. hard cheese, shredded

1 red onion, sliced

8 fresh basil leaves

1 medium tomato

1 teaspoon salt

2 tablespoons mayonnaise

1 teaspoon dried dill

1/2 cup milk of choice

2 egg whites

Directions

Preheat oven to 450 degrees F. Prepare non-stick baking tray.

Spread mustard over 4 bread slices. Then layer cheese, onion slices, basil leaves, and tomato slices. Season with salt.

Sprinkle dried dill and spread mayonnaise over bread. Top with remaining bread slices.

Whisk milk and eggs in a mixing bowl. Season with salt if desired. Soak bread slices in the milk-egg mixture.

Transfer sandwiches to the baking tray, and bake 10 minutes or until your sandwiches become golden brown.

Refreshing Quinoa Salad

(Ready in about 25 minutes | Servings 6)

Ingredients

1 cup quinoa

2 teaspoon olive oil

2 medium onions, finely chopped

1 tablespoon fresh ginger, minced

1 tablespoon balsamic vinegar

1½ cups carrot, shredded

1 teaspoon salt

1/4 teaspoon black pepper

1/4 teaspoon paprika

1/4 cup chopped walnuts

1 cup cooked peas, drained and rinsed

1 medium apple, diced

1/3 cup unsweetened coconut, shredded

Directions

Heat oil in a wide saucepan and sauté onion until tender. Add minced ginger, quinoa, vinegar, and carrots. Season with salt, pepper and paprika, stirring frequently. Bring the mixture to a boil.

Cover the saucepan, reduce heat to medium, and simmer 20 minutes, or until liquid is evaporated.

Toast walnuts in a pan over medium heat 3 to 5 minutes, or until they begin to brown, stirring frequently. Cool the walnuts.

Add peas on top of the prepared quinoa. Set aside for 5 minutes, till peas are warmed through.

Add apple slices and scatter coconut and walnuts over your salad. Serve immediately.

Fruity Family Breakfast

(Ready in about 15 minutes | Servings 4)

Ingredients

1 medium watermelon

1 honeydew

1 cup Red grapes, seedless

1 Green grapes, seedless

4 peaches, peeled and diced

16 skewers

Directions

Cut watermelon in halves and place upside down on a large serving platter.

Cut remaining watermelon and honeydew into bite-sized cubes.

Thread fruit bites onto skewers and insert them into the watermelon half.

Fruits will be beautifully decorated. In this way, you will willingly eat fruit, especially the children will be happy.

Honey Lentil Loaves

(Ready in about 1 hour 40 minutes | Servings 12)

Ingredients

2 packages of yeast

1/2 cup warm water

8 cup all-purpose flour

4 ¼ cup barley flour

2 ½ cup soy flour

1 cup lentils, cooked and mashed

4 teaspoons honey

4 tablespoons butter, melted

1 1/2 cup warm water

Directions

Preheat the oven to 375 degrees F. Butter a loaf pan.

Dissolve the yeast in the 1/2 cup of warm water and set aside for 10 minutes.

     Combine flours.

Blend lentils, honey, butter and 1/2 cup water in an electric blender or a food processor.

Add remaining water (1 cup) and the mixed flours to lentil mixture. Add the yeast mixture.

Transfer it on floured surface and knead several times. Let the dough rise until it is doubled in size.

Knead once again and form into four loaves. Place into buttered loaf pan.

Bake in the middle of the oven for 50 minutes to 1 hour, or until loaves are well browned and a toothpick inserted in the center of loaf comes out clean.

Quick Tropical Oatmeal

(Ready in about 15 minutes | Servings 1)

Ingredients

1/4 cup quick oats

1/4 cup diced fresh mango

1/3 cup water

1/8 teaspoon allspice

1 teaspoon honey

Toasted coconut shredded (optional)

Directions

Cut mango into bite-sized pieces.

Pour in water, and add mango in a medium saucepan. Bring to boil and add oats and allspice, and cook for about 7 minutes.

Remove from the heat and add honey. Scatter the coconut if desired.

Serve hot with milk on the side.

Figs Carrot Loaf

(Ready in about 2 hours | Servings 12)

Ingredients

1 package of yeast

3 cups pastry flour

2 teaspoon honey

1/2 teaspoon cinnamon

3/4 cup warm water

1 cup carrots, shredded

1/2 cup figs, chopped

Milk (optional)

Directions

Sift 1 cup of flour in a large bowl and add yeast, honey, and cinnamon. Add water and beat a few minutes with electric mixer.

Stir in carrots, figs, and remaining flour to make a soft dough.

Transfer the dough to floured surface and knead until elastic.

Cover and let rise in a warm place until the dough is doubled in size.

Transfer the dough to floured surface, and roll dough to 7 x 12 inches.

Place in the oiled loaf pan. Cover, let rise for another 1 hour. Set oven rack to the middle position and bake your loaf for 30 minutes. Cool on a wire rack before cutting and serving.

Cut into thin slices and serve at room temperature, with hot milk.

Toasted Bread with Homemade Prune Spread

(Ready in about 1 hour 10 minutes | Servings 12)

Ingredients

3/4 pound prunes, pitted

2 cups water

1/2 cup orange juice

2 tablespoons lemon juice

2 cups sugar

1/2 teaspoon salt

1/2 teaspoon cinnamon

Toasted bread

Directions

Combine prunes, water, orange juice, lemon juice, sugar, salt and cinnamon in a large saucepan and bring to a boil. Reduce the heat to medium-low and simmer for 30 minutes.

Blend the mixture in the blender and return it to the saucepan. Simmer for 20 minutes more, till the mixture is thick.

Cool the mixture for 10 minutes. If the mixture is too watery, cook an additional 10 minutes.

Let it cool and divide among glass jars. Serve with toasted bread or scones of choice.

Keep in a refrigerator for a few months.

Berry Oatmeal with Almonds

(Ready in about 10 minutes | Servings 2)

Ingredients

1/2 cup quick rolled oats

1 cup milk

1 cup frozen mixed berries

1/4 teaspoon cinnamon

1/8 teaspoon almond extract

1 tablespoon brown sugar

Toasted almonds for garnish

Directions

Mix oats and milk in a large and deep saucepan.

Cook over medium heat till mixture comes to a boil or for 3 minutes. Reduce the heat and simmer for another 3 minutes, stirring occasionally.

Add prepared berries, cinnamon, almond extract and sugar and heat through. Taste and adjust the seasonings.

Sprinkle chopped almonds and serve hot.

Homemade Cinnamon Rolls

(Ready in about 2 hours | Servings 18)

Ingredients

4 tablespoons butter

1 cup brown sugar

1 teaspoons cinnamon

1 teaspoon allspice

2 cups all-purpose flour

2 tablespoons sugar

2 teaspoons baking powder

2 teaspoons baking soda

1 teaspoon salt

3 tablespoons butter, softened

3/4 cup milk

confectioners' sugar for garnish

Directions

To make the filling: Mix softened butter, sugar, cinnamon and allspices in a large mixing bowl.

Spread 1/2 of the mixture in a baking pan.

To make the dough: Sift flour, and add sugar, baking powder, baking soda and salt. Pour in milk to form a dough, and cut in softened butter.

Preheat the oven to 400 degrees F.

Roll out dough on a floured surface and form a rectangle.

Spread the remaining filling all over the dough. Roll up dough and then pinch edge together to seal. Cut the dough into 18 small rolls.

Bake for 25 minutes. Remove from the oven and sprinkle confectioners' sugar.

Healthy Grain Fruit Breakfast

(Ready in about 25 minutes | Servings 8)

Ingredients

2 cups multi-grain flakes

2 cups oatmeal

2 tablespoons wheat germ

1 tablespoons cinnamon

1/4 teaspoon grated nutmeg

1/2 cup yogurt

1 cup unsweetened applesauce

1/4 cup honey

1 tablespoon maple syrup

1 egg

1/2 cup milk powder

2 teaspoon baking powder

1/2 cup cranberries

Directions

Preheat oven to 350 degrees F. Prepare a non-stick cookie sheet.

Crush multi-grain flakes in a medium bowl. Add oatmeal, wheat germ, cinnamon and grated nutmeg. Reserve.

Whisk together yogurt, applesauce, honey, maple syrup, beaten egg, and milk powder.

Add baking powder to the wet mixture and mix to combine all ingredients.

Add the dry mixture to the wet mixture and stir well. Add cranberries and stir well.

Form the mixture into 24 balls and lightly flatten them. Place onto the cookie sheet. Bake for about 15 minutes.

Pita Bread with Tzatziki and Boiled Eggs

(Ready in about 25 minutes | Servings 6)

Ingredients

1/2 medium cucumber, peeled	1/4 teaspoon salt
1 cup yogurt	1 teaspoon fresh parsley
2 cloves garlic, minced	Pita bread triangles
1 tablespoon fresh dill, minced	6 boiled eggs

Directions

Slice the cucumber in half lengthwise and discard seeds.

Grate the cucumber and place into a clean cotton kitchen towel. Gently squeeze out all the liquid from the cucumber. Place the prepared cucumber in a serving bowl.

Stir in the yogurt, garlic, dill, and salt. Chill for at least 30 minutes before serving.

Garnish with chopped fresh parsley and serve with pita bread triangles and boiled eggs.

English Muffins with Tempeh and Sauce

(Ready in about 35 minutes | Servings 4)

Ingredients

5 tablespoons vegetable stock

2 tablespoons soy sauce

2 teaspoons liquid smoke

2 tablespoons pure maple syrup

2 tablespoon mustard

1 teaspoon sea salt

1/4 teaspoon black pepper

8 ounces tempeh, divided into 4 patties

2 tablespoons olive oil

1/2 onion, finely chopped

1/4 cup mayonnaise

2 tablespoons nutritional yeast

2 tablespoons white wine vinegar

vegetable oil, for cooking

2 English muffins, split and toasted

2 cups baby arugula

1 red bell pepper, sliced

Directions

To make the marinade: Combine the stock, soy sauce, liquid smoke, maple syrup, and mustard. Mix to combine and season with salt and pepper.

Marinade the tempeh overnight, refrigerated.

Heat the olive oil in an iron-skillet over medium-high heat. Sauté the onion for 5 minutes, or until it is soft and translucent.

Transfer to a food processor or an electric blender, and add the mayonnaise, nutritional yeast, and wine vinegar.

Process until the mixture is smooth. Taste and adjust the seasonings. Blend once again.

Heat a thin layer of cooking oil in a wide and deep saucepan over medium-high heat. Place the tempeh in the heated saucepan. Cook 5 minutes until browned. Gently flip and cook on the second side, for 5 minutes.

Arrange English muffins on a plate, add baby arugula, 1 tempeh patty, and slices of red pepper.

Top with the sauce and serve.

Crispy-Soft Filo Triangles

(Ready in about 50 minutes | Servings 12)

Ingredients

1 tablespoon olive oil

2 medium onions, finely chopped

2 cups semihard cheese of choice

6 tablespoons butter, melted

Salt to taste

8 sheets filo dough (12 x 16 inches)

Directions

Heat the oil in a wide saucepan and sauté the onions until tender and translucent, about 10 minutes. Transfer to a small bowl and set aside.

Preheat the oven to 400 degrees F. Prepare a non-stick baking sheet or line a baking sheet with parchment paper.

Place the 8 sheets filo dough on surface and cover them with a wax paper, then cover with a damp kitchen towel to prevent the filo dough from drying out.

Remove 1 sheet from the stack, cover again, and lightly brush the dough with melted butter. Layer a second sheet of filo. Brush it with butter. Cut the sheets of filo into 3 equal strips.

Cut cheese into small cubes. Place 1 tablespoon cheese cubes and onion near the corner of strip. Carefully make triangles. Create a triangle so that the filling cannot drop out. You can make 12 triangles.

Lightly brush the triangles with melted butter, and then transfer them on the baking sheet. Season with salt if desired.

Bake for 15 minutes, or until the triangles are golden. Serve immediately.

Classic French Toast

(Ready in about 20 minutes | Servings 3)

Ingredients

6 thick slices bread

2 eggs

2/3 cup milk

1 teaspoon salt to taste

1/4 teaspoon ground cinnamon

1/4 teaspoon ground nutmeg

Directions

Beat eggs, milk, salt, cinnamon, and nutmeg.

Soak each slice of bread in egg-milk mixture.

Heat a lightly oiled cast-iron skillet over medium-high heat.

Place the bread slices in the heated cast-iron skillet, and cook on both sides until golden. Serve hot with milk or yogurt.

PART TWO LUNCH

Zucchini Soup with Baby Spinach

(Ready in about 25 minutes | Servings 6)

Ingredients

2 tablespoons canola oil

1 yellow onion, diced

1 zucchini, cut into bite-sized cubes

2 cups vegetable broth

2 cups water

1 (15-ounces) can brown beans, rinsed and drained

4 cups baby spinach leaves

2 tablespoon lemon juice

2 tablespoons mint leaves, chopped

1 teaspoon salt

1/2 teaspoon black pepper

1 teaspoon dried basil

Directions

Heat oil in a wide and deep saucepan over medium-high heat. In a hot oil, sauté onion, stirring often, 3 to 5 minutes, or until translucent and tender.

Add the zucchini and cook until vegetables are well browned and tender.

Add vegetable broth and 2 cups water, and bring to a boil.

Drain and rinse beans and add to saucepan. Add spinach leaves, reduce heat to medium, and simmer 5 minutes. Add lemon juice and mint leaves.

Season with salt and pepper, add basil and serve hot.

Cauliflower-Cheese Soup

(Ready in about 35 minutes | Servings 8)

Ingredients

1 tablespoon olive oil

1 onion, chopped

1 large head cauliflower, trimmed and roughly chopped

3 cups vegetable stock

2 cups water

1/4 teaspoon ground cumin

1/4 cup milk

2 tablespoons butter

1 teaspoon salt

1/2 teaspoon black pepper

1/3 cup Swiss cheese, grated

Directions

Heat olive oil in a wide and deep saucepan over medium-high heat. Sauté onion in saucepan until tender, stirring often. Add cauliflower, vegetable stock, and water, and bring to a boil.

Stir in cumin and reduce heat, and simmer for 20 minutes, or until vegetables are tender.

Purée soup in a blender or a food processor, until smooth, and return to the saucepan.

Stir in milk and butter and cook for a few minutes more. Season with salt and pepper, and divide among serving plates. Sprinkle with grated cheese and serve immediately.

Chickpea Stew with Couscous

(Ready in about 35 minutes | Servings 8)

Ingredients

2 tablespoons canola oil

4 green onions, chopped

1 carrot, diced

1 parsnip, diced

1 red bell pepper, sliced

2 (16-ounces) cans chickpeas, rinsed and drained

1 (32-ounces) container squash soup

1 teaspoon salt

1/2 teaspoon freshly ground black pepper

1 teaspoon dried dill

2 cups couscous, cooked

Directions

Heat canola oil in a large and wide saucepan over medium-high flame. Add onion, carrot and parsnip, and sauté 5 to 6 minutes, or until vegetables are tender.

Add bell pepper, and sauté 3 to 5 minutes more, or until tender and fragrant. Add bay leaf.

To make Purée: Process 3/4 cup chickpeas and 3/4 cup squash soup in a blender until smooth. Add purée to carrot-parsnip mixture and combine with remaining chickpeas and soup.

Reduce the heat to medium-low and simmer for 20 minutes. Season with salt and pepper. Add dill, taste and adjust the seasonings.

Fluff cooked couscous with a fork and divide among serving bowls. Ladle the stew over couscous and serve immediately.

Mexican Chili-Enchilada Stew

(Ready in about 35 minutes | Servings 4)

Ingredients

2 tablespoons butter, melted

1 yellow onion, finely chopped

2 cloves garlic, minced

1 (19 ounce) can green enchilada sauce

1 ½ cups water

1 cube vegetable stock

1/4 teaspoon chili powder

1/4 teaspoon cumin, ground

1 (15 ounce) can beans, drained and rinsed

4 medium tomatoes, peeled and blended

1 Jalapeño pepper, finely chopped

1 cup corn kernels

4 corn tortillas, torn into strips

1 teaspoon salt

1 teaspoon black pepper

Directions

Heat the butter in a skillet. Sauté onions and garlic until soft.

In a large stockpot, mix the enchilada sauce and water. Add vegetable stock, chili powder, and cumin. Bring to a boil.

Reduce heat to medium-low. Stir in the beans, tomatoes, jalapeño and corn. Simmer for 10 to 12 minutes.

Tear the tortillas into strips, add to the stew and cook for a few minutes. Season with salt and pepper and serve warm.

Spiced Vegetables and Rice with Cashews

(Ready in about 25 minutes | Servings 4)

Ingredients

4 tomatoes, diced

1 onion, chopped

2 tablespoons fresh ginger, minced

2 tablespoons olive oil

1 teaspoon garam masala

3 tablespoons dried cranberries

2 cups green beans

2 cups zucchini

3/4 cup chickpeas

6 tablespoon milk of choice

1 teaspoon fine sea salt

1 cup brown rice, cooked

3 tablespoons cashews, toasted

Directions

Purée tomatoes, onion, and ginger in a food processor or a blender.

Heat olive oil in a large skillet over medium-heat. Add garam masala and cook 30 seconds.

Add tomato purée and cranberries. Cook until sauce is thickened.

Mix in green beans, zucchini and chickpeas. Stir in milk and season with salt. Cover, reduce heat to medium-low, and simmer until vegetables are tender.

Serve prepared vegetables over rice. Scatter cashews and serve immediately.

Lentil-Chickpea Stew with Currants

(Ready in about 40 minutes | Servings 6)

Ingredients

2 tablespoons canola oil

1 large yellow onion, chopped

3 cloves garlic, minced

4 medium tomatoes, peeled and blended

4 cups cooked lentil soup

1 (15-ounces) can chickpeas, rinsed and drained

1/2 cup dried currants

1 tablespoon cumin, ground

1 teaspoon salt

1/2 teaspoon black pepper

1/4 teaspoon paprika

2 bay leaves, crushed

Boiled potato for garnish (optional)

Directions

Heat canola oil in a wide saucepan over medium-high heat. Sauté onion, stirring occasionally, until tender. Add garlic, and cook 1 to 2 minutes more.

Stir in tomatoes, lentil soup, chickpeas, currants, and cumin. Season with salt and pepper, add paprika and bay leaves.

Reduce the heat and simmer over medium heat, stirring occasionally. Simmer for about 30 minutes, or until sauce is thickened, stirring frequently.

Serve over boiled potatoes if desired.

Thick Bean and Potato Soup

(Ready in about 1 hour | Servings 4)

Ingredients

2 tablespoons olive oil

3 large onions, finely chopped

3 cloves garlic, minced

2 medium potatoes, peeled and diced

3 carrots, shredded

1 celery, shredded

4 cups water, divided

1 ½ cups tomato purée

1 head roasted garlic

1 teaspoon cayenne pepper

1/2 teaspoon basil

2 1/2 cups kidney beans, drained and rinsed

1 teaspoon salt

1/2 teaspoon freshly ground black pepper

Directions

Heat the oil in a stockpot over medium heat. Add the onion, garlic, potatoes, carrots, and celery. Cook for 5 minutes, stirring occasionally, until the vegetables are just tender.

Add 3 cups of the water and tomato purée.

Blend the remaining 1 cup of water and the roasted garlic in a food processor, until smooth. Add to the soup and bring to a boil. Reduce the heat, add cayenne pepper and basil and simmer for 30 minutes longer.

Stir in the beans and simmer 15 minutes more over medium heat. Season with salt and pepper.

Serve immediately.

Tahini and Chickpea Broth

(Ready in about 35 minutes | Servings 4)

Ingredients

1 tablespoon toasted sesame oil

1 onion, chopped

2 cloves garlic, crushed

1/2 teaspoon paprika

2 cups chickpeas, cooked

Juice from one fresh lemon

3 ½ cups vegetable broth

1/2 cup tahini

1 teaspoon salt

1/2 teaspoon black pepper

1/4 cup parsley, roughly chopped

Directions

Heat the oil in a wide and deep stockpot. Add the onion, garlic, paprika, and chickpeas. Cook on medium heat, stirring frequently, for about 6 minutes. Add the lemon juice and mix to combine.

Add the broth to the stockpot and bring to a boil. Reduce the heat, cover and simmer, for 10 minutes. Stir in tahini, and simmer for 5 minutes longer.

Purée the soup. You can use a handheld blender or any regular blender. Season with salt and black pepper.

Divide among serving bowls, garnish with parsley and serve warm.

Quick Cheese Soup

(Ready in about 25 minutes | Servings 4)

Ingredients

2 tablespoons olive oil

1 bunch green onions, chopped

3 cloves garlic, crushed

2 teaspoons grated fresh ginger

1 ½ cup Cheddar cheese, grated

½ cup daikon matchsticks

1 large carrot, grated

1 small parsnip, grated

1 teaspoon kosher salt

¼ teaspoon ground white pepper

¼ teaspoon paprika

2 ½ cups vegetable broth

3 tablespoons soy sauce

Directions

Heat the oil in a wide saucepan or a wok over medium-high heat. Add the onions, garlic, and ginger. Cook for 3 to 5 minutes, until fragrant and just tender.

Add the cheese, daikon, carrot, and parsnip. Season with salt, pepper, and paprika. Cook for 2 minutes, stirring occasionally.

Add the broth and soy sauce, lower the heat to medium-low and simmer for 15 to 20 minutes.

Serve immediately.

Vegetarian-style 'Bolognese'

(Ready in about 35 minutes | Servings 4)

Ingredients

- 2 tablespoons extra-virgin olive oil
- 4 spring onions, chopped
- 3 garlic cloves, peeled and chopped
- 3 large tomatoes, peeled and blended
- 2 cups canned tomato purée
- 2 cups water
- 1 teaspoon salt
- 1/2 teaspoon black pepper
- 1 teaspoon dried basil
- 1 teaspoon dried rosemary
- 1 tablespoon Italian Seasoning mix
- 2 large carrots, shredded
- 4 large mushrooms, sliced
- 1 package spaghetti for 4 people
- 1/2 cup Parmesan cheese
- 1/2 teaspoon red pepper flakes for garnish

Directions

Heat the oil in a wide and deep saucepan over medium-high heat. Sauté the onions and garlic until soft and translucent. Stir in the blended tomatoes and tomato purée, lower the heat to medium and cook for 5 minutes, or until heated through.

To make the sauce: Pour in the water and add salt, pepper, basil, rosemary and Italian Seasoning mix.

Bring to a boil, then reduce the heat and simmer for 5 to 6 minutes. Process the sauce in a blender until smooth.

Add the grated carrots and sliced mushrooms to the saucepan and simmer until the sauce is thickened and reduced.

Cook the spaghetti according to instructions on a package.

Ladle sauce over spaghetti, top with parmesan cheese and sprinkle red pepper flakes. Serve warm.

Spanish Vegetable Paella

(Ready in about 50 minutes | Servings 4)

Ingredients

- 1 cup long-grain white rice
- 2 cups hot water
- 1 tablespoon canola oil
- 1 yellow onion, chopped
- 3 cloves garlic, minced
- 2 green bell peppers, sliced
- 1 tomato, diced
- 2 cups vegetable stock
- 1 teaspoon salt
- 1/2 teaspoon black pepper
- 1 teaspoon cayenne pepper
- 1 teaspoon turmeric
- 1 cup peas
- 1 cup artichoke, cut into chunks

Directions

Bring a pot of water to a boil, and cook the rice for 30 minutes.

Heat the oil in a wide saucepan or a wok over medium flame. Sauté the onion and garlic until the onion is soft. Add the peppers and tomato and continue cooking for 5 minutes more.

Add the rice and stock. Bring to a boil, then lower the heat and simmer. Season with the salt, black pepper, cayenne pepper and turmeric. Cover with a lid and cook for 10 minutes more.

Add the peas and artichoke and cook until the vegetables are just tender. Serve immediately.

Spinach Cannelloni with Béchamel

(Ready in about 1 hour | Servings 4)

Ingredients

- 1 ½ cups cannelloni tubes
- 3 cups spinach, blanched and chopped
- 2 tablespoons olive oil
- 2 cups homemade arrabbiata sauce
- 4 tablespoons butter
- 3 tablespoons all-purpose flour
- 2 cups hot milk
- 2 bay leaves
- 1 teaspoon salt
- 1/4 teaspoon black pepper
- 1/4 teaspoon freshly grated nutmeg
- 1 cup made breadcrumbs

Directions

Preheat the oven to 350 degrees F. Oil ovenproof dish with 1 tablespoon olive oil.

Gently stuff the cannelloni tubes with the chopped spinach.

Spread half of the arrabbiata sauce evenly over the bottom of the ovenproof dish. Place the stuffed cannelloni and pour over the remaining half of the arrabbiata sauce.

To prepare béchamel sauce: Melt the butter in a saucepan over a medium-high flame. Add the flour and mix well. Pour in the hot milk, stirring constantly. Add bay leaves, salt, pepper and grated nutmeg. Allow to cook for 2–3 minutes.

Pour the béchamel sauce over the cannelloni to cover pasta evenly.

Top with breadcrumbs and drizzle the remaining olive oil.

Cover the dish with a foil and bake for 30 minutes. Then uncover and bake for 20 minutes longer.

Creamed Mushroom Tagliatelle

(Ready in about 1 hour | Servings 4)

Ingredients

3 spring onions, chopped

3 garlic cloves, chopped

2 cups baby spinach

1 cup mushrooms, sliced

1 teaspoon sea salt

1/4 teaspoon black pepper

1 basil

1/2 cup heavy cream

1 packet tagliatelle of choice, for 4 people

Parmesan cheese for garnish

Directions

In a wide and deep saucepan, sauté the onion and garlic until tender and translucent. Add the spinach and mushrooms, and cook until the mushrooms are tender and fragrant.

Season with salt, pepper and basil and stir through. Add heavy cream, lower the heat and simmer for 10 minutes, until the cream is thickened.

Prepare tagliatelle according to instructions on the package. Divide the pasta among serving plates. Pour prepared sauce over tagliatelle and scatter Parmesan cheese. Serve immediately.

Creamy Spiced Tomatoes

(Ready in about 30 minutes | Servings 4)

Ingredients

8 ripe tomatoes

1 tablespoon fresh basil

1 tablespoon fresh rosemary

1 teaspoon fresh dill

4 garlic cloves, minced

1 teaspoon salt

1/2 black pepper

1 cup heavy cream

2 tablespoons olive oil

6 tablespoons breadcrumbs

Directions

Preheat the oven to 350 degrees F. Slightly oil a deep ovenproof dish.

Cut the tomatoes in halves and place in the ovenproof dish. Sprinkle the fresh basil, rosemary and dill.

Scatter the minced garlic over the tomatoes. Season with salt and black pepper.

Pour in the heavy cream. Drizzle with olive oil and then top with breadcrumbs.

Bake for 20 minutes until the dish is golden and crispy.

Chilled Summer Soup

(Ready in about 15 minutes | Servings 4)

Ingredients

1 large cantaloupe, seeded and chilled

2 tablespoons orange juice

1 tablespoon lemon zest

Salt (optional)

Freshly ground black pepper (optional)

lemon wedges for garnish

mint leaves for garnish

Directions

Cut the cantaloupe into bite-sized chunks.

To make the fine purée: Process the cantaloupe chunks in an electric blender or food processor. Add the orange juice and lemon zest, and blend until all ingredients are well combined.

Season with salt and black pepper if desired.

Garnish with lemon wedges and mint and serve chilled.

Broccoli Rabe with Cheese

(Ready in about 45 minutes | Servings 4)

Ingredients

1 pound broccoli rabe, washed and trimmed

4 tablespoons canola oil

1 medium onion, finely chopped

1 clove garlic, minced

1/2 teaspoon kosher salt

1/4 teaspoon black pepper

Cheese of choice, for garnish

Directions

Bring a large pot of water to a boil over medium-high heat. Cook broccoli rabe in the boiling and salted water. Cook until the vegetables are just tender, do not overcook. Drain and set aside.

Heat canola oil in a wide saucepan and sauté onion and garlic until the onion is translucent and tender. Season with salt and pepper.

Stir in the broccoli rabe and cook for 15 minutes. Garnish with cheese and serve over boiled potatoes or cooked brown rice.

Two-Bean Chili with Cheese

(Ready in about 25 minutes | Servings 6)

Ingredients

2 tablespoons olive oil

1 onion, diced

2 cloves garlic, minced

4 large tomatoes, diced

1 (15 ounce) can kidney beans, drained

1 (15 ounce) can chili beans

1 teaspoon salt

1/2 teaspoon freshly ground black pepper

1 (12 ounce) package vegetarian burger crumbles

1 cup hard cheese, shredded

Directions

Heat olive oil in a cast-iron skillet and sauté the onion and garlic. Sauté until the onions are translucent and soft, or for 5 to 6 minutes.

In a deep and wide stockpot stir in the tomatoes, beans and prepared onion and garlic. Bring the stockpot to a boil over medium-high heat. Season with salt and pepper.

Lower heat to medium-low, mix in the burger crumbles and cook until heated through.

Divide prepared chili beans among serving bowls, scatter shredded cheese of choice and serve immediately.

Baked Asparagus in Sauce

(Ready in about 25 minutes | Servings 4)

Ingredients

1 bunch asparagus, trimmed

Non-stick cooking spray

1 teaspoon fine sea salt

1/2 teaspoon black pepper

1/2 teaspoon red pepper flakes

3 tablespoons butter

2 tablespoon tamari sauce

1 tablespoon lemon juice

Directions

Preheat oven to 400 degrees F. Slightly oil a baking sheet.

Place the asparagus on the baking sheet. Sprinkle salt, black pepper and red pepper.

Bake asparagus 10 to 12 minutes until just soft.

Melt the butter in a skillet over medium-low heat. Stir in tamari sauce and lemon juice. Pour the sauce over the baked asparagus and serve immediately.

Buttery Carrots with Basmati Rice

(Ready in about 30 minutes | Servings 4)

Ingredients

1 pound baby carrots, peeled

1/4 cup butter

1/3 cup brown sugar

Salt to taste

2 cups cooked basmati rice

Directions

Bring a large pot of water to a boil. Cook the baby carrots in a boiling water over medium-high flame until tender. Drain the carrots and reserve.

Drain off liquid, leaving a small amount of water in a pot.

Stir in butter and brown sugar into the water. Reduce the flame to medium and simmer for a few minutes.

Return prepared carrots to the pot and toss. Season with salt if desired.

Serve over basmati rice.

Summer Stuffed Tomatoes with Pesto

(Ready in about 1 hour | Servings 4)

Ingredients

1 (16-ounce) can brown beans, drained and rinsed

1/2 cup Pesto

1 teaspoon salt

1/4 freshly ground pepper to taste

1/4 ground white pepper

1 onion, finely chopped

1/2 head roasted garlic, chopped

1/2 celery rib, finely chopped

4 large ripe tomatoes

Parsley for garnish

Directions

To prepare the filling: Combine the beans in a large bowl with Pesto. Season with salt, black pepper and white pepper.

Add onion, garlic and celery. Chill the filling until cold.

Cut off the top of each tomato and discard pulp with a spoon. Place the tomatoes onto a serving platter,

Stuff the tomatoes with chilled filling. Garnish with parsley and serve immediately.

Rice Zucchini-Tomato Casserole

(Ready in about 1 hour | Servings 6)

Ingredients

1/3 cup basmati rice

2/3 cup water

2 tablespoons olive oil

1 ½ pounds zucchini, diced

1 red onion, chopped

2 cloves garlic, minced

1 salt

1/2 teaspoon black pepper

1/2 teaspoon basil

1/2 teaspoon cayenne pepper

1 1/2 cups ripe tomatoes, seeded and diced

2 cups hard cheese of choice, grated

Directions

Bring a large pot of water to a boil over medium-high heat. Stir in the rice into boiling water, reduce heat to low, and simmer 20 minutes, until rice is soft.

Preheat oven to 350 degrees F. Oil a casserole dish.

Heat the oil in a wide and deep saucepan over medium-high heat, and cook the zucchini, onions, and garlic, stirring occasionally. Cook until the vegetables are tender. Season with salt, black pepper, basil, and cayenne pepper.

Stir in the cooked rice and tomatoes. Cook until heated through. Transfer to the oiled casserole dish. Top with cheese and cover with a foil. Bake for 20 minutes, or until the cheese is golden.

Chilled Picnic Soup

(Ready in about 25 minutes + chilling | Servings 6)

Ingredients
10 ripe plums
1/2 cup red wine
1/2 cup water
1/4 teaspoon ground coriander
1/4 teaspoon ground cinnamon
1 teaspoon salt
1 tablespoon molasses
1/2 cup heavy cream
1 cup sour cream

Directions

Bring a deep and wide saucepan of water to a boil. Blanch the plums in a boiling water. Peel the plums and discard the pits. Set aside.

Place the plum skins in the saucepan and combine with the red wine and 1/2 cup water. Cook for 5 minutes.

Remove the plum skins and place in a strainer. Press out liquid and after that discard the skins.

Cut plums into a small pieces. Stir in the plums in the wine mixture. Add coriander, cinnamon, salt, and molasses. Simmer for 10 minutes.

To prepare purée: blend the prepared mixture with the heavy cream. Transfer to a large bowl and chill until the soup is very cold.

Mix in the sour cream and stir well to combine. Serve chilled.

Baked Spiced Zucchini and Potatoes

(Ready in about 1 hour 10 minutes | Servings 6)

Ingredients
2 medium zucchini
4 large potatoes
1 medium green bell pepper, seeded and chopped
2 cloves garlic, minced
1/2 cup dry bread crumbs
1/4 cup canola oil
1 teaspoon salt
1 teaspoon ground black pepper
1/2 teaspoon cayenne pepper

Directions

Preheat oven to 400 degrees F. Grease a baking tray.

Cut zucchini into the large chunks. Peel potatoes and cut into large chunks too.

In the prepared baking tray, combine the zucchini, potatoes, green bell pepper, garlic, bread crumbs, and canola oil. Season with salt, pepper and cayenne pepper. Mix well to combine all ingredients.

Bake 1 hour, stirring occasionally, until the vegetables are tender and crispy.

Chilled Yogurt Cucumber Soup with Almonds

(Ready in about 1 hour 10 minutes | Servings 4)

Ingredients

3 cups plain yogurt

1/2 cup water

2 cucumbers

2 tablespoons extra-virgin olive oil

1 tablespoon balsamic vinegar

2 cloves garlic, minced

1 tablespoon dried dill

1 teaspoon salt

Freshly ground pepper to taste

1/2 cup almonds, toasted and finely chopped

Directions

Whisk together the yogurt and water.

Peel the cucumbers and slice them in halves lengthwise. Spoon the seeds and discard them. Cut the cucumbers into bite-sized chunks and add to the yogurt mixture.

Add vinegar, garlic, dill, salt and pepper, and stir well.

Chill for about 1 hour before serving. Divide among serving bowls, scatter toasted and chopped almonds and serve chilled.

Iced Cucumber and Watercress Soup

(Ready in about 30 minutes + chilling | Servings 6)

Ingredients

2 tablespoons butter

2 white onions, finely chopped

4 cucumbers, peeled

2 cups Vegetable broth

1 teaspoon dried tarragon

1 teaspoon balsamic vinegar

1 teaspoon salt

1/2 teaspoon freshly ground black pepper

1 bunch watercress, patted dry

1 cup sour cream

Directions

Melt the butter in a wide cast-iron skillet over medium-high heat. Sauté the onions until tender and translucent.

Cut the cucumbers into halves and discard the seeds by using the spoon. Cut into small chunks.

In a large stockpot mix the cucumber chunks, vegetable broth, tarragon and vinegar. Season with salt and pepper and stir well. Cover the stockpot and bring to a boil.

Cook over medium heat for 20 minutes, stirring occasionally, until the cucumber chunks are tender.

Tear off watercress leaves from their stems and discard the stems. Mince the leaves and reserve.

Purée the cooked soup in a food processor until smooth. Transfer the soup into a serving bowl and stir in watercress leaves.

Stir in the sour cream. Chill the soup at least 4 hours before serving.

Mushrooms Pasta Casserole

(Ready in about 45 minutes | Servings 6)

Ingredients

1 (8 ounce) package pasta
2 tablespoons olive oil
1/2 pound mushrooms, thinly sliced
1/2 cup margarine
1/4 cup whole wheat flour
2 large cloves garlic, minced
1/2 teaspoon dried basil
1 teaspoon oregano
1 teaspoon salt
1/4 teaspoon black pepper
2 cups milk
1 cup mozzarella cheese, grated
1 (10 ounce) package frozen chopped spinach, thawed
1/4 cup tamari sauce
Parsley for garnish

Directions

Preheat oven to 350 degrees F. Oil a baking casserole dish.

Bring a pot of salted water to a boil. Cook pasta 10 minutes, until al dente. Drain and set aside.

Heat the oil in a wide skillet over medium-high heat. Cook the mushrooms, for a few minutes or until soft.

To prepare sauce: Heat and melt margarine in a saucepan. Stir in flour, garlic, basil, and oregano. Season with salt and pepper. Gradually mix in the milk until the sauce is thickened.

Stir in cheese until melted. Stir in cooked pasta, mushrooms, spinach, and tamari sauce. Transfer to the oiled casserole dish and bake for 20 minutes.

Let sit for 10 minutes before serving. Sprinkle parsley and serve warm.

Mom's Creamy Cheesy Cabbage

(Ready in about 1 hour 20 minutes | Servings 6)

Ingredients

1/2 cup olive oil
4 onions, chopped
4 cloves garlic, minced
2 bay leaves
3 cups baby carrots, sliced
1 medium cabbage, shredded
2 medium potatoes, diced
2 cups Vegetable Stock
2 teaspoons soy sauce
4 tablespoons butter
1/2 teaspoon dried thyme
1 teaspoon salt
1/4 teaspoon freshly ground black pepper
1 teaspoon cayenne pepper
1 jalapeño, minced
12 slices French bread
3 cups Swiss cheese, shredded

Directions

In a wide and deep pot heat the oil over medium heat. Add the onions, garlic, and bay leaves, and sauté for 10 minutes, stirring occasionally. Add the carrots and cook for 10 minutes longer.

Add shredded cabbage, potatoes, vegetable stock, soy sauce and butter. Season with thyme, salt, black pepper, and cayenne pepper. Add minced jalapeño.

Bring to a boil, then lower the heat and simmer for about 1 hour, or until the vegetables are soft.

Toast slices of French bread under the broiler.

Put 2 slices of French bread in each serving bowl. Ladle the cabbage soup over it. Then scatter shredded Swiss cheese and serve.

Creamy Yam Soup

(Ready in about 40 minutes | Servings 6)

Ingredients

3 cups Vegetable broth	1 teaspoon salt
5 yams, peeled and diced	1/2 teaspoon freshly ground black pepper
3/4 cup whipping cream	1/2 teaspoon paprika
4 tablespoons margarine	1/2 red pepper flakes
1/4 cup dry sherry	

Directions

Heat a large saucepan over medium-high heat. Mix the vegetable broth and yams in the saucepan, bring to a boil, and cook until the vegetables are soft, or for about 20 minutes.

Blend cooked mixture in a food processor until smooth. Return it to the saucepan. Stir in whipping cream, 2 tablespoons margarine, sherry, salt, black pepper and paprika.

Divide soup among serving bowls, dot with margarine and serve immediately.

Exotic Curried Stew with Coconut Milk

(Ready in about 40 minutes | Servings 6)

Ingredients

- 3 tablespoons olive oil
- 2 red onions, finely chopped
- 1 jalapeño, seeded and minced
- 3 cloves garlic, minced
- 1 tablespoon fresh ginger, minced
- 1 teaspoon ground coriander
- 1 teaspoon turmeric
- 1 teaspoon salt
- 1/4 teaspoon freshly ground black pepper
- 1 cup sliced mushrooms
- 3 cups Vegetable Stock
- 2 cups canned coconut milk
- 2 potatoes, peeled and diced
- 1½ cups egg noodles
- 2 cups small cauliflower, broken into small florets
- 1 tablespoon balsamic vinegar

Directions

In a medium cast-iron skillet, heat the olive oil and add the onions and jalapeño. Sauté for 5 to 6 minutes, or until the onions are translucent. Add the garlic, ginger, coriander and turmeric and cook for 3 minutes, stirring constantly.

Season with salt and black pepper. Stir in the mushrooms until soft and fragrant, then add the vegetable stock and coconut milk.

Bring the content to a boil. Add the potatoes and cook for 10 to 12 minutes, stirring often, until the potatoes are soft.

Add the egg noodles, bring to a boil, and add the cauliflower florets and balsamic vinegar. Cook, stirring frequently, or until the noodles are just tender.

Divide among serving bowls and serve warm.

Greens and Potatoes Casserole

(Ready in about 50 minutes | Servings 6)

Ingredients

1 (10 ounce) package frozen greens

6 potatoes, peeled and chopped

1/2 cup butter

1 cup sour cream

1 tablespoon onion, chopped

2 cloves garlic, minced

1 teaspoon salt

1/4 teaspoon dried dill

1 teaspoon basil

1 cup shredded Cheddar cheese

Directions

Preheat oven to 350 degrees F. Grease a casserole dish.

Cook greens according to package instructions.

Bring a large stockpot to a boil. Place potatoes and cook for 15 minutes, or until they are just tender but firm. Drain, cool enough to handle and mash.

Mix the greens, mashed potatoes, butter, sour cream, onion, garlic, salt, dill, and basil. Place to the prepared casserole dish. Top with Cheddar cheese.

Bake for 20 minutes, until cheese is bubbly and golden.

Chickpea and Ginger Stew with Yogurt

(Ready in about 40 minutes | Servings 4)

Ingredients

1/4 cup canola oil

2 medium onions, diced

3 cloves garlic, minced

2 tablespoons fresh ginger, minced

2 teaspoons coriander, minced

1/4 teaspoon cayenne pepper

1 (15-ounce) can chickpeas, drained and rinsed

1 (16-ounce) can diced tomatoes

1 medium carrot, diced

1 medium potato, diced

1 teaspoon salt

1/4 teaspoon white pepper

4 cups water

3 tablespoons butter

Lemon wedges for garnish

1 cup Yogurt for garnish

Directions

In a wide and deep saucepan, heat the oil over medium-high flame. Sauté the onions, garlic, ginger, coriander, and cayenne pepper, stirring often, until the onions are translucent and tender.

Stir in the chickpeas, tomatoes, carrot, and potato. Season with salt and pepper, add water and cook for 30 minutes, or until the vegetables are soft.

Swirl in the butter, taste and adjust the seasonings.

Ladle into bowls, garnish with a lemon wedges. Serve with yogurt on the side.

Quick Asparagus Frittata

(Ready in about 25 minutes | Servings 4)

Ingredients

2 tablespoons olive oil

3 green onions, minced

1/2 teaspoon salt

1/4 teaspoon black pepper

1 pound asparagus

6 large eggs

1/2 cup Swiss cheese, shredded

Directions

Heat the oil in a medium saucepan over medium-high heat. Sauté the onions, stirring occasionally, until they become tender.

Season with salt and pepper. Reduce the heat to medium-low, then add the asparagus, and continue cooking for another 3 minutes.

Pour the lightly beaten eggs in the saucepan and cook until set.

Add shredded cheese, cut Frittata into 4 portions and divide among serving plates.

Chickpeas in Cream Sauce

(Ready in about 20 minutes | Servings 4)

Ingredients

2 cups chickpeas

2/3 cup vegetable stock

1/2 teaspoon salt

1/4 teaspoon ground white pepper

1/2 teaspoon dried dill

3 tablespoons butter

1/3 cup heavy cream

2 tablespoons all-purpose flour

Directions

In a wide saucepan, combine chickpeas, vegetable stock, and salt. Bring to a boil, and then season with pepper and dill. Stir in butter.

To make the cream: Whisk together cream and flour in a medium mixing bowl. Pour the cream over chickpeas.

Cook for 5 to 6 minutes more. Garnish with dill and serve warm.

Vegetables with Cheese and Pumpkin Seeds

(Ready in about 45 minutes | Servings 4)

Ingredients

1 large eggplant

5 tablespoons oil

2 medium onions, diced

4 cloves garlic, minced

1 (16-ounce) can diced tomatoes, well drained

1 (16-ounce) can chickpeas, drained and rinsed

1 teaspoon fine sea salt

1/4 teaspoon freshly ground black pepper

1 teaspoon basil

semi-hard cheese of choice, shredded

fresh parsley, roughly chopped

pumpkin seeds, toasted

Directions

Preheat the oven to 350 degrees F.

Peel the eggplant and cut into bite-sized cubes.

Heat 3 tablespoons of the oil in a wide saucepan over medium-high heat. Fry the eggplant cubes, stirring occasionally, until just tender. Heat 1 tablespoon oil and fry the remaining eggplant cubes.

Transfer the eggplant cubes to the serving platter.

Put 1 remaining tablespoon of oil in the saucepan and sauté the onions and garlic until the onions are tender and translucent, for about 5 minutes.

Drain the tomatoes well. Drain the chickpeas. Stir in the tomatoes and cook for 5 minutes. Add the chickpeas and eggplant and stir well to combine ingredients.

Season with salt, pepper and basil, and cook 5 minutes.

Transfer the meal to a baking dish and bake for 10 minutes. Scatter your favorite cheese and return to the oven for 10 minutes longer. Sprinkle fresh parsley and pumpkin seeds and serve warm.

Quick Fried Spiced Corn

(Ready in about 25 minutes | Servings 4)

Ingredients

4 ears corn

2 tablespoons butter

1 yellow onion, sliced

1 teaspoon garlic salt

1/2 teaspoon ground black pepper

1/2 teaspoon paprika

Directions

Remove corn kernels from the cobs.

Melt and heat butter in a wide saucepan over medium flame. Cook the corn kernels just until soft and heated through.

Stir in onion. Continue cooking until the onion becomes crispy. Season with garlic salt, pepper, and paprika.

Stuffed Tomatoes with Cheese and Almonds

(Ready in about 50 minutes | Servings 4)

Ingredients

4 medium ripe tomatoes

2 scallions, finely chopped

2 tablespoon fresh parsley, finely chopped

1/2 cup feta cheese, crumbled

1/4 cup bread crumbs

3 tablespoons extra-virgin olive oil

1/4 cup almonds, toasted and chopped

Rosemary for garnish

Olives for garnish, pitted

Directions

Cut off top of each tomato. Scoop out pulp and seeds. Discard seeds. Save the pulp and chop it.

Preheat oven to 350 degrees F. Grease a baking pan.

To make the filling: Combine tomato pulp, scallions, parsley, feta cheese, bread crumbs, olive oil, and almonds.

Stuff the tomatoes. Layer tomatoes right side up in the baking pan. Bake for about 15 minutes, or until the tomatoes are tender and heated through.

Sprinkle rosemary and serve with olives.

Potato and Onion Broth

(Ready in about 1 hour | Servings 5)

Ingredients

3 potatoes, peeled and sliced

3 medium yellow onions, thinly sliced

3 (10-ounce) cans vegetable stock

1 cup water

1/2 cup heavy cream

2 tablespoons butter

1 teaspoon salt

1/2 teaspoon black pepper

Parsley for garnish

Directions

Place potatoes, onions, vegetable stock, and water in a wide and deep stockpot. Bring to a boil over medium-high flame.

Lower heat and simmer 40 minutes, or until potatoes are soft.

Mash cooked potatoes and onions with a vegetable masher until they are smooth.

Stir in heavy cream, butter, salt, and black pepper.

Cook soup for a few minutes longer. Divide among serving bowls, sprinkle parsley and serve with toasted bread on the side.

Veggie BBQ with Soy Marinade

(Ready in about 1 hour + marination time 1 hour | Servings 4)

Ingredients

1/4 cup soy sauce	1 cup firm tofu
2 tablespoons sugar	1 red bell pepper
1 tablespoon fresh ginger, grated	1 green bell pepper
8 wooden skewers	1 cup mushrooms
1 cup cauliflower florets	1 cup onion
1/2 cup cherry tomatoes	Salt to taste
1 medium zucchini	Black pepper to taste

Directions

To make the marinade: Whisk soy sauce, sugar, and ginger.

To prepare skewers: Soak them in a water for 30 minutes.

Cut vegetables and tofu into bite-sized cubes. Thread vegetables and tofu cubes onto skewers.

Place skewers in a shallow bowl and pour marinade over them. Marinate at least 2 hours at room temperature.

Preheat outdoor or indoor grill.

Remove skewers from the marinade and grill them for about 10 minutes, turning occasionally, until heated through.

Replace skewers to a serving platter. Season vegetables with salt and pepper if desired. Taste and adjust the seasonings.

Pour in the remaining marinade and serve warm.

Fava Beans with Herbs and Tomatoes

(Ready in about 45 minutes | Servings 4)

Ingredients

2 eggs	3 tablespoons olive oil
1 (18-ounces) can fava beans	1 teaspoon salt
3 cloves garlic, crushed	1/4 teaspoon pepper
2 tablespoons fresh parsley, chopped	1/2 teaspoon cayenne pepper
1 tablespoon rosemary	2 lime, cut into wedges
2 tomatoes, chopped	

Directions

Place eggs in a deep saucepan and cover them with enough water.

Place the saucepan over medium heat until boiling, then lower heat and simmer for 15 minutes. Run cold water over eggs until they are chilled.

Peel cooked eggs. Rinse and set aside.

Drain and rinse beans. Place fava beans in the saucepan and cook over medium heat for 7 to 8 minutes.

Add eggs, garlic, parsley, rosemary, tomatoes, and olive oil. Season with salt, pepper and cayenne pepper.

Divide beans among serving bowls. Garnish with lime wedges and serve warm.

Greens with Herbs and Yogurt

(Ready in about 30 minutes | Servings 4)

Ingredients

6 cups mixed kale	1/2 head garlic, crushed
6 cups broccoli rabe	1 teaspoon salt
1 cup parsley, chopped	1/4 teaspoon black pepper
3 tablespoons olive oil	lemon wedges for garnish
2 teaspoons cayenne pepper	yogurt (optional)
2 teaspoons ground cumin	

Directions

Discard kale stems and tough ribs. Place the greens and parsley in a steamer and cook until soft and wilted.

Chop cooked greens into pieces and reserve.

Heat the oil in a large saucepan over medium heat and add cayenne pepper and cumin. Stir in garlic and greens and cook until liquid is evaporated.

Season with salt and pepper, taste and adjust the seasonings.

Transfer prepared dish into a serving bowl and garnish with lemon wedges. Serve with yogurt if desired.

Garlicky Jerusalem Artichokes in Wine Sauce

(Ready in about 30 minutes | Servings 4)

Ingredients

2 tablespoons vegetable oil

1 pound Jerusalem artichokes, sliced

2 garlic cloves, minced

1 teaspoon salt

1/4 teaspoon freshly ground black pepper

1 tablespoon rosemary

1 teaspoon basil

1/4 teaspoon grated nutmeg

1/2 cup dry white wine

Directions

Heat the oil in a wide and deep saucepan. Sauté the artichokes and garlic until the vegetables are tender and fragrant.

Season with salt and black pepper.

Add rosemary, basil, nutmeg and wine. Cook over medium-high heat until the wine is almost absorbed. Serve warm.

Kohlrabi with Horseradish and Sour Cream

(Ready in about 15 minutes | Servings 4)

Ingredients

4 medium kohlrabi peeled

4 tablespoons sour cream

horseradish in vinegar

2 teaspoons dill

1 teaspoon kosher salt

1/2 teaspoon black pepper

Directions

Cut the kohlrabi into julienne strips. Steam 5 to 8 minutes, or until soft.

Transfer to a serving bowl and toss with the sour cream.

Add horseradish and dill. Season with salt and pepper. Serve immediately.

Baked Mushrooms with Almonds

(Ready in about 35 minutes | Servings 4)

Ingredients

1 pound cremini mushrooms, sliced

1 teaspoon salt

1/4 teaspoon freshly ground black pepper

3 tablespoons olive oil

3 tablespoons parsley, chopped

1 teaspoon dried dill

1 teaspoon dried basil

2 garlic cloves, mince

4 tablespoons toasted almonds

Directions

Preheat the oven to 400 degrees F.

In a baking dish, layer the sliced mushrooms, drizzle olive oil and season with salt and pepper.

Sprinkle parsley, dill, basil and garlic, and bake until sizzling, about 25 minutes.

Scatter the almonds and serve warm.

Pasta with Caramelized Scallions and Walnuts

(Ready in about 1 hour | Servings 6)

Ingredients

4 tablespoons olive oil

3 pounds scallions

1 teaspoon sea salt

1/4 teaspoon black pepper

1 cup dry white wine

3 tablespoon walnuts, toasted and roughly chopped

Pasta of choice

Directions

Heat the oil in a large saucepan over medium heat. Sauté the scallions, stirring frequently, and cook for 5 to 6 minutes.

Reduce the heat, add the wine, cover and cook 30 minutes, or until the scallions are golden brown. Stir occasionally. Season with salt and black pepper.

Meanwhile, cook your favorite pasta according to instructions, drain and set aside.

Pour caramelized onions over cooked pasta. Scatter the walnuts and serve warm.

Curried Parsnips with Chutney

(Ready in about 35 minutes | Servings 4)

Ingredients

1½ pounds parsnips, peeled

3 tablespoons butter

1 red onion, thinly sliced

2 apples, cored

1 teaspoon curry powder

1 teaspoon salt

1/4 teaspoon milled pepper

1/4 cup yogurt

1/4 cup Apple-Pear Chutney

2 tablespoons cilantro, chopped

Directions

Steam the parsnips until tender, or for 7 minutes. Slice the parsnips and apples into bite-sized chunks.

Melt butter in a medium cast-iron skillet. Sauté the onion for 5 minutes.

Add apples and curry powder and cook over medium heat. Then add the parsnips and continue cooking.

Season with salt and pepper, and cook 5 minutes more. Remove the saucepan from the heat, then stir in the yogurt and chutney.

Sprinkle the cilantro and serve warm.

Stir-Fried Peas and Carrots with Sichuan Pepper Salt

(Ready in about 25 minutes | Servings 6)

Ingredients

2 tablespoons canola oil

1 garlic clove, chopped

1 pound snow peas

2 carrots, shredded

1 teaspoon Sichuan Pepper Salt

1 teaspoon dried dill

Rice optional

Directions

Heat canola oil in a wide and deep skillet. Add the garlic and sauté for 1 to 2 minutes.

Add the peas and carrots and stir-fry until they are tender. Season with the pepper salt and toss.

Add dried dill, taste and adjust the seasonings. Serve over rice.

Italian Juicy Peperonata

(Ready in about 35 minutes | Servings 4)

Ingredients

1/4 cup canola oil

2 onions, sliced

3 garlic cloves, minced

2 bay leaves

2 red bell peppers, sliced

2 yellow bell peppers, sliced

2 green bell peppers, sliced

1 teaspoon salt

1/4 teaspoon black pepper

4-5 peppercorns

5 ripe tomatoes, peeled, seeded and sliced

Semi-soft cheese of choice to garnish

Directions

Heat the canola oil in a wide saucepan. Add the onions, garlic, bay leaves, and cook over medium-high heat, stirring constantly, until the onions are tender and translucent, about 10 minutes.

Add the peppers and continue cooking. Season with salt, pepper and peppercorns. Cook until the peppers begin to tender.

Stir in the tomatoes and reduce the heat to medium-low. Continue to simmer, stirring often, for 15 minutes.

Transfer prepared peperonata to a serving platter, garnish with favorite cheese and serve warm.

Three-Peppers Tomato Stew

(Ready in about 30 minutes | Servings 4)

Ingredients

3 tablespoons olive oil

3 red onions, diced

1 garlic clove, minced

2 pounds tomatoes, peeled, seeded, and chopped

2 red bell peppers

2 yellow bell peppers

1 green bell pepper

3 teaspoons Harissa

1 teaspoon salt

1/4 black pepper

1 tablespoon basil

Directions

Heat olive oil in a large saucepan. Sauté the onions until tender and translucent.

Add the garlic, tomatoes, peppers, and harissa. Season with salt, pepper and basil.

Simmer for a few minutes, stirring occasionally, until the sauce is thickened, or about 25 minutes. Taste and adjust the seasonings.

Divide among serving plates and serve hot.

PART THREE DINNER

Fresh Vegetable Spring Rolls

(Ready in about 1 hour | Servings 4)

Ingredients

2 green onions, finely chopped

3 garlic cloves, minced

2 large carrots, grated

4 large zucchini, grated

1 teaspoon fine sea salt

1/4 teaspoon black pepper

1/4 teaspoon red pepper flakes

1 teaspoon basil

16 spring spring roll wrappers

Cooking oil for deep-frying

Dipping Sauce of choice

Directions

Heat 1 tablespoon oil in a wok or a wide saucepan. Sauté the onions and garlic until the onion is tender and translucent.

Stir in the carrots and zucchini and cook until they are tender, or 10 minutes.

Turn off the heat and add salt, black pepper, red pepper flakes and basil. Set aside to cool before preparing the roll wrappers.

Lay out the spring wrappers and place them on a damp towel or a bamboo sushi mat.

Working quickly, place two tablespoons of the vegetable mixture into the centre of prepared roll wrapper. Fold in the sides, then roll the wrapper over until it obtains a cylindrical shape.

Reserve and cover with a damp towel or a bamboo sushi mat. Repeat with each successive wrapper.

Heat the oil in a deep saucepan to deep-fry the wrappers. Fry until they are crisp and golden. Serve immediately with your favorite Dipping Sauce.

Crunchy Pea Bites

(Ready in about 1 hour | Servings 6)

Ingredients

1 ½ cup cooked snow peas

1 cup chana flour

1 teaspoon baking powder

1 yellow onion, chopped

2 chillies, seeded and finely chopped

2 cups raw kale, chopped

1 teaspoon salt

1 teaspoon cayenne pepper

1 cup water

vegetable oil for deep-frying

Directions

Mash cooked snow peas. Combine pea puree with flour, baking powder, onion, chillies and kale. Season with salt and pepper and mix well to combine all ingredients.

Add the water, then mix to a doughy consistency.

Heat the oil in a wide heavy skillet. Drop spoonfuls of the mixture into the hot oil.

Deep-fry the bites until they are golden. When they are ready, drain them on a roller towel.

Vegetarian Sausages with Vegetables

(Ready in about 35 minutes | Servings 4)

Ingredients

2 tablespoons canola oil

6 medium potatoes, diced

6 vegetarian sausages

1 large red bell pepper

1½ cups Brussels sprouts, thinly sliced

1 cup vegetable broth

2/3 cup shallot, chopped

1 cup button mushrooms, chopped

1 teaspoon salt

1/2 teaspoon freshly ground black pepper

2 cloves garlic, minced

1 tablespoon minced fresh thyme

Directions

Heat the oil in a wide and deep skillet over medium heat. Add the potatoes and cook for 10 to 12 minutes, stirring occasionally, until browned.

Add the sausages and cook for 5 to 7 minutes until browned. Add the bell pepper and Brussels sprouts. Cook for 4 to 6 minutes until the vegetables are just tender.

Add a broth, the shallot, and mushrooms. Season with salt and pepper. Cook for 3 minutes until the shallots are tender.

Turn off the heat. Stir in the garlic and thyme. Taste and adjust the seasonings. Serve warm with cooked macaroni if desired.

Easy Seitan Burgers

(Ready in about 25 minutes | Servings 4)

Ingredients

2/3 cup ketchup

1 cup apple cider vinegar

3 tablespoons mustard

2 tablespoons molasses

2 tablespoons barbecue sauce

1 teaspoon fine sea salt

2 teaspoon freshly ground black pepper

12 oz. seitan

4 burger-style buns

8 Butter lettuce leaves

3 pickles, optional

Directions

Combine ketchup, vinegar, mustard, molasses, barbecue sauce, salt and pepper in a wide saucepan. Bring the mixture to a simmer over medium-high heat. Cook 5 minutes.

Pour in sauce to a bowl.

Cut the seitan into thin strips. Place seitan to a saucepan, and cook 10 minutes, until the seitan strips heated through.

Divide seitan mixture among buns. Layer lettuce leaves, sliced pickles and prepared sauce. Serve immediately.

Spicy Salad with Peanut Dressing and Croutons

(Ready in about 20 minutes | Servings 6)

Ingredients

3 green onions, chopped

1 large cucumber, peeled and sliced

2 cups cabbage, finely shredded

1 cup fresh bean sprouts

2 small carrots, thinly sliced

2/3 cup crunchy natural peanut butter

3 tablespoons milk

2 tablespoons lemon juice

1 tablespoon lemon zest

2 cloves garlic, minced

1 teaspoon brown sugar

1 teaspoon fine sea salt

1/4 teaspoon freshly ground black pepper

1/4 teaspoon red pepper flakes

4 tablespoons water

Croutons of choice

Directions

To make the salad: Place the onions, cucumber, cabbage and bean sprouts in a large mixing bowl and toss.

To make the dressing: Whisk the peanut butter and milk (e.g. with a fork) until well blended. The dressing should be very thick at this moment.

Add lemon juice, lemon zest, garlic, sugar, salt, black pepper, red pepper and water, and mix well to combine all ingredients. Taste and adjust the seasonings.

Divide the prepared salad among the serving plates. Top with the dressing and garnish with the slices of carrot. Serve with your favorite croutons.

Rutabaga and Carrot Gratin

(Ready in about 40 minutes | Servings 4)

Ingredients

1 medium rutabaga (about 2 pounds)

1 large carrot

3 tablespoons butter

1 teaspoon salt

1/4 teaspoon freshly ground black pepper

1 cup heavy cream

1/4 cup Bread Crumbs of choice

Directions

Peel the rutabaga and cut it into chunks. Shred the rutabaga chunks in a food processor.

Peel and grate the carrot.

Melt 2 tablespoons of the butter in a large cast-iron skillet over medium-high flame. Sauté the rutabaga and carrot for 10 minutes, stirring constantly.

Preheat the oven to 375 degrees F.

Butter a baking dish and add prepared mixture. Season with the salt and pepper.

Pour on the heavy cream, coating evenly the mixture. Sprinkle the bread crumbs and add the remaining tablespoon of butter. Bake for 25 minutes, or until the heavy cream is thickened. Serve immediately.

Stir-Fried Asparagus with Tofu and Chestnuts

(Ready in about 20 minutes | Servings 4)

Ingredients

2 tablespoons soy sauce

2 tablespoons water

3 tablespoons dry sherry

2 teaspoons cornstarch

2 cups asparagus

1/4 cup peanut oil

1 pound firm tofu, cut into cubes

1 tablespoon water

1 large green bell pepper, seeded and sliced

1 can (8-ounce) water chestnuts, rinsed and drained

1 ½ cup brown rice, cooked

A few drops Tabasco

Red pepper flakes for garnish

Directions

Combine the soy sauce, water, sherry, and cornstarch in a mixing bowl. Reserve.

Cut off the bottoms of the asparagus. Cut the asparagus at the diagonal into 2-inch lengths.

Heat the peanut oil in a wok over high flame. Add the tofu, and stir-fry until golden, about 8 minutes. Remove the tofu from the wok. Reserve.

Reduce the heat to medium, add the asparagus and 1 tablespoon of water in the heated wok. Cover and cook until the asparagus is tender.

Drain and rinse chestnuts. Add the green bell pepper and water chestnuts in the wok. Stir-fry for 3 minutes.

Return the tofu to the wok and toss. Stir in the soy sauce mixture and cook 1 to 2 minutes.

Remove from the flame and sprinkle Tabasco sauce. Serve over cooked brown rice and garnish with red pepper flakes.

Braised Tofu and Veggies in Sauce

(Ready in about 35 minutes | Servings 4)

Ingredients

1/4 cup canola oil

2 cups firm tofu, patted dry

2 white onions, chopped

1 tablespoon garlic, minced

3 cups button mushrooms, sliced

1½ cups tomatoes (from 28-ounce can), minced and drained

1/3 cup dry white wine

1 teaspoon tamari sauce

1/4 cup vegetable stock

1/2 teaspoon paprika

1 teaspoon salt

1/2 teaspoon freshly ground black pepper

2 tablespoons leeks for garnish

Directions

Heat the oil in a wide saucepan or a wok over medium-high heat. Cut the tofu into bite-sized cubes. Add the tofu cubes and stir-fry until it is golden. Set aside.

Heat the oil in a saucepan and sauté the onions and garlic until the onions are translucent and soft. Add the mushrooms and sauté, stirring frequently, for 10 minutes.

Add the drained tomatoes and reserved tofu and stir well.

To make the sauce: Mix wine, tamari sauce, vegetable stock, paprika, salt and pepper. Stir to combine all ingredients well.

Pour the sauce over the tofu mixture. Reduce the heat and simmer for 10 minutes. The sauce should be thickened. Garnish with chopped leeks and serve immediately.

Mango and Avocado Light Salad

(Ready in about 15 minutes | Servings 4)

Ingredients

2 green onions, finely chopped

1 mango, peeled

1 avocado, peeled

2 chillies, finely chopped

8-10 leaves Romaine lettuces

3 tablespoons lemon juice

1 tablespoon apple cider vinegar

2 tablespoons olive oil

1 teaspoon fine sea salt

1/2 teaspoon black pepper

1 tablespoon fresh parsley

Directions

Cut the mango and avocado into bite-sized cubes. Place avocado and mango cubes into a medium serving bowl. Add the chopped green onions and chillies.

Tear the lettuce leaves with your fingers. Add lettuce strips in the bowl.

Drizzle the lemon juice, vinegar and olive oil. Season with salt and pepper. Garnish with parsley and serve immediately.

Lentil and Broccoli Salad with Chilli and Coriander

(Ready in about 15 minutes | Servings 4)

Ingredients

2 cups brown lentils, cooked

1 onion, thinly sliced

1/2 cup broccoli, blanched and broken into florets

1 fresh red chilli, seeded thinly sliced

10 olives, pitted

juice of 1 fresh lemon

1/4 cup extra-virgin olive oil

1 teaspoon fine sea salt

1/4 teaspoon black pepper

1 tablespoon fresh basil

2 tablespoons fresh coriander, roughly chopped

fresh lemon wedges for garnish

Directions

Slice the onion into small rings. Squeeze the lemon and reserve.

Place the cooked lentils onto a serving plate and top with the onion rings.

Add the broccoli florets, chilli and olives.

Drizzle with lemon juice and olive oil. Taste and adjust the seasonings. Scatter chopped coriander, garnish with lemon wedges and serve immediately.

Pita Bread with Greek Salad

(Ready in about 15 minutes | Servings 4)

Ingredients

ripe tomatoes

1 large cucumber

1 green bell pepper

1 red bell pepper

1 medium red onion

15 calamata olives

3 tablespoons extra-virgin olive oil

1 teaspoon salt

1/2 teaspoon black pepper

handful of fresh dill, chopped

3/4 cup Feta cheese, crumbled

4 pita bread

Directions

Slice the tomatoes and cucumber into bite-sized chunks.

Slice the peppers and cut the onion into small rings. Combine the vegetables and add the olives.

Drizzle the oil and add salt and pepper. Gently stir to combine all ingredients. Scatter Feta cheese on top of prepared salad.

Taste and adjust the seasonings. Divide the salad among serving bowls and sprinkle chopped dill. Serve with hot pita bread.

Quick French Bread Pizza

(Ready in about 15 minutes | Servings 2)

Ingredients

1 French demi-baguette

1/4 cup pesto sauce

1/2 cup mozzarella, shredded

1/3 cup roasted tomatoes

1 teaspoon oregano

1 teaspoon basil

6 black olives, pitted

Ketchup (optional)

Directions

Preheat oven to 350 degrees F. Butter a baking sheet and set aside.

Cut the bread into halves lengthwise. Place bread on the baking sheet.

Top each half with pesto, cheese and tomatoes. Sprinkle oregano and basil. Season with salt if desired.

Bake for 10 minutes, until cheese is melted. Cool 5 minutes before serving. Serve warm with ketchup of choice.

Indian Vegetable Bondas

(Ready in about 40 minutes | Servings 6)

Ingredients

4 tablespoon canola oil

2 cups Potato buds

2 teaspoons sea salt

1 cup hot water

1 teaspoon mustard seed

1 teaspoon ginger, grated

2 large green chilies, chopped

1 small bunch coriander leaves, chopped

1 yellow onion, finely chopped

1 cup peas

1/2 cup shredded carrots

1 teaspoon lime juice

1 cup gram four

1/2 teaspoon baking powder

Cooking oil for deep-frying

Directions

Mix potato buds with water and add the salt.

Heat 2 tablespoons oil in a wide saucepan over medium-high heat and add mustard seeds.

Add ginger, chilies, coriander leaves, and onion and sauté until onions are tender.

Reduce the heat and add carrots and peas. Cook for about 10 minutes.

Add mashed potatoes and cook for another 5 minutes.

Remove from heat, add lime juice and let cool.

To prepare batter: Combine gram flour, 2 tablespoons oil, 3/4 cup water, salt to taste and the baking powder and mix well.

Form small balls from the potato mixture and roll them in the batter.

Heat the cooking oil in a large saucepan. Deep-fry balls until they are golden brown. You can prepare about 25 bondas.

Chilli-Coriander Rice

(Ready in about 35 minutes | Servings 4)

Ingredients

1/2 cup basmati rice

3 fresh green chillies, seeded

2 cloves garlic

3 handfuls of fresh coriander, finely chopped

3 tablespoons canola oil

1 teaspoon cumin seeds

1 teaspoons kosher salt

Directions

Chop the chillies, garlic and coriander together using a pestle and mortar in order to make a fine paste. Rinse and drain the rice.

Heat the oil in a large saucepan over a medium heat, and add the cumin seeds. When the seeds begin to brown, stir in the rice, paste and salt.

Pour in 4 cups of boiling water and stir.

Increase the heat to high and boil for 7–8 minutes, stirring often, until the water is absorbed.

Cover the pan, reduce the heat to the low setting and simmer for 10 minutes. Remove from the heat and let it stand for 15 minutes before serving.

Italian Tomato-Rosemary Bruschetta

(Ready in about 20 minutes | Servings 8)

Ingredients

1 Italian bread,

2 garlic clove, minced

2 tablespoon extra-virgin olive oil

2 tomatoes, peeled, and chopped

1/4 teaspoon sea salt

1/4 teaspoon black pepper

2 tablespoons fresh rosemary

2 tablespoons oregano

Directions

Cut the bread into thin slices.

Toast the bread slices under the broiler until they are lightly browned.

Mix the garlic and olive oil and brush the slices of bread with that mixture.

Spread the tomatoes over the bread slices. Season with salt and pepper. Broil for a few minutes. Sprinkle with rosemary and oregano and serve immediately.

Italian-style Pasta Salad

(Ready in about 30 minutes + chilling time | Servings 4)

Ingredients

1 (16 ounce) package fusilli pasta

1 cup mayonnaise

1/2 cup sour cream

1 (7 ounce) package Italian-style salad dressing mix

1 cup chickpeas, cooked

2 (2 ounce) cans black olives

4 scallions, chopped

2 tablespoons fresh parsley, chopped

Directions

In a stockpot of salted boiling water, cook fusilli pasta until al dente. Rinse pasta and drain. Let stand to cool.

Combine mayonnaise, sour cream and Italian dressing mix in a mixing bowl. Whisk all ingredients until smooth. Reserve.

In a salad bowl combine pasta, peas, olives, and scallions. Pour in the prepared dressing and let sit at least 3 hours in a refrigerator.

Stir before serving and sprinkle the parsley.

Avocado Salad Bowl with Corn Chips

(Ready in about 20 minutes | Servings 4)

Ingredients

1 avocado, peeled and pitted

1/2 cup mayonnaise

1/4 teaspoon Tabasco sauce

1/4 cup extra-virgin olive oil

1 clove garlic, minced

1/2 teaspoon kosher salt

1 head butter lettuce, torn into small pieces

3 ounces hard cheese of choice, shredded

2 tomatoes, diced

2 scallionss, chopped

10 olives, pitted

1 cup coarsely crushed corn chips

Directions

Process avocado, lemon juice, mayonnaise, tabasco sauce, olive oil, garlic, and salt in a blender. Blend until smooth.

In a large salad bowl, combine together romaine lettuce, cheese, tomatoes, scallions, olives, and corn chips.

Add the avocado dressing before serving.

Bucatini and Asparagus with Sauce

(Ready in about 35 minutes | Servings 2)

Ingredients

1 ½ cups Bucatini pasta

1/2 bunch asparagus, trimmed and cut into 3/4-inch pieces

1 teaspoon olive oil

2 tablespoons garlic, minced

/4 cup whole milk

1/8 teaspoon salt

1/4 teaspoon freshly ground black pepper

1 teaspoon basil

1 teaspoon minced fresh tarragon, or 1/4 teaspoon dried

1 tablespoon dry white wine

1/2 cup Parmesan cheese, shredded

Directions

Bring a large pot of water to a boil. Cook pasta for 5 minutes.

Add asparagus and cook, until the pasta and asparagus are soft. Drain the pasta and asparagus and set aside.

Heat oil in a cast-iron skillet over medium flame. Sauté garlic until fragrant, or 1 minute. Four in the milk and season with salt, pepper and basil. Bring to a simmer, and cook until the mixture is thickened. Stir in tarragon and wine.

Add the prepared sauce into the cooked pasta and cook over medium flame. Cook, stirring often for 5 minutes.

Top with the Parmesan cheese and serve immediately.

Quick Vegetable Tagine

(Ready in about 40 minutes | Servings 2)

Ingredients

1 tablespoon canola olive oil

1 medium onion, chopped

1 cup red bell pepper, seeded and diced

1/4 teaspoon caraway seeds

1 teaspoon salt

1/8 teaspoon cayenne pepper

2 cloves garlic, minced

2 cups tomato pasta

1 (8-ounce can) chickpeas, rinsed

1/4 teaspoon black pepper

2 large eggs

1/4 teaspoon red pepper flakes

Directions

Heat oil in a wide and deep saucepan over medium-high heat. Sauté onion, stirring constantly, until translucent. Add sliced red bell pepper and cook until tender and fragrant.

To prepare spice mixture: Process caraway seeds and salt in a blender or grind them in a mortar and pestle. Add cayenne pepper.

Add garlic and the spice mixture to the saucepan and cook briefly for 1 minute.

Add tomatoes and chickpeas, reduce heat to medium and simmer until thickened. Add black pepper, taste and adjust the seasonings.

Break eggs into the saucepan, reduce heat to medium-low and cook the eggs for 5 to 6 minutes Sprinkle prepared meal with red pepper flakes and serve immediately.

Crustless Cauliflower-Cheese Pie

(Ready in about 1 hour | Servings 4)

Ingredients

- 3 tablespoons grated Parmesan cheese
- 1/4 cup Bread Crumbs
- 1/4 cup cottage cheese
- 1/4 cup milk
- 1 cup semi-soft cheese
- 3 eggs, well beaten
- 2 cups cauliflower broken into small florets
- 1 tablespoon minced fresh basil
- 1 teaspoon fresh dill
- 1 teaspoon salt
- 1/4 teaspoon freshly ground black pepper
- 1/4 teaspoon smoked paprika
- 1 tablespoon butter, melted

Directions

Preheat the oven to 350 degrees F. Butter a baking pie plate.

To make a crust: Combine the Parmesan cheese and bread crumbs and place onto the bottom of the pie plate. Reserve.

Cut cottage cheese into small cubes. Beat the eggs. Mix the cottage cheese, milk, cheese, and eggs together. Stir in cauliflower florets, basil, dill, salt, black pepper and paprika.

Pour prepared mixture over pie crust. Dot a pie with butter.

Bake for 40 minutes, until a knife inserted in the center of the pie comes out clean.

Cut the pie into slices, divide among serving plates and serve immediately.

Buttermilk Onion Tart

(Ready in about 40 minutes | Servings 8)

Ingredients

- 1 can (8 oz) refrigerated crescent dinner rolls
- 1 white onion, chopped
- 2 tablespoons butter
- 4 eggs
- 1½ cups buttermilk
- 2 cloves garlic, minced
- 2 teaspoons chopped fresh rosemary leaves
- 1/4 teaspoon dried thyme
- 1/4 teaspoon dried tarragon, crumbled
- 1 teaspoon salt
- 1/2 teaspoon black pepper
- 2 tablespoons brown sugar
- 1½ cups soft French cheese (e.g. Muenster cheese), grated

Directions

Preheat the oven to 375 degrees F.

Melt 1 tablespoon of the butter in a wide saucepan, and sauté the onions, until soft and translucent.

To prepare filling: Beat the eggs in a large mixing bowl, then beat in the buttermilk. Add garlic, rosemary, thyme, tarragon, salt and pepper. Stir in brown sugar.

Place the grated cheese over the pie crust evenly, then layer the prepared filling. Top with remaining tablespoon of butter.

Bake until a knife or toothpick inserted in the center comes out clean and dry. Let cool on a wire rack for 20 minutes before cutting and serving. Serve warm.

Eggplant and Tomato Tart with Herbs

(Ready in about 1 hour | Servings 6)

Ingredients

1/3 pound puff pastry

3 cups eggplant, sliced

4 tablespoons olive oil

4 cloves garlic, crushed

1 tablespoon fresh basil

1 tablespoon fresh dill

3 tablespoon bread crumbs

3 cups tomatoes, peeled and sliced

1/2 teaspoon salt

1/4 teaspoon black pepper

Directions

Preheat the oven temperature to 375 degrees F. Line a baking sheet with parchment paper.

Stretch and roll out the pastry into a round shape and let stand in a refrigerator.

Toss the eggplant slices in a bowl and drizzle the olive oil. Cook eggplant slices in a non-stick pan, until they are golden and cooked through.

Combine garlic, basil, dill and bread crumbs.

Place chilled puff pastry on the baking sheet. Layer eggplant slices and tomato slices over pastry.

Season with salt and pepper and adjust the seasonings. Top with garlic and herbs mixture.

Bake for 35 minutes. Cool on a wire rack before serving.

Cornmeal Bean and Tomato Pie

(Ready in about 1 hour | Servings 6)

Ingredients

2½ cups water

1½ cups cornmeal

½ teaspoon salt

3 tablespoons canola oil

2 medium onions, diced

1 red bell pepper, seeded and diced

1/2 teaspoon ground cumin

1 can (16-ounce) tomatoes, diced

1 can (16-ounce) kidney beans

1 cup corn, fresh

1 teaspoon salt

1/4 teaspoon freshly ground black pepper

1 cup semi-soft cheese, grated

1 tablespoon butter

Directions

Preheat the oven to 350 degrees F. Butter a pie plate.

To prepare the crust: Heat a wide saucepan over medium heat. Place the water, cornmeal, and salt in a saucepan. Bring to a boil, stirring frequently, until the mixture is smooth. Cook 5 to 6 minutes.

Heat the oil in a cast-iron skillet over medium-high heat. Add the onions and bell pepper, and cook until soft and fragrant, for about 10 minutes.

Add the cumin, tomatoes and beans, and toss well. Cook until the mixture is heated through. Add the corn, salt, and pepper and cook for 1 to 2 minutes longer.

Distribute 2/3 of the cornmeal on the pie plate. Top with the tomato and bean mixture. Layer the cheese.

Top with the remaining dough for crust and spread evenly. Spread evenly 1 tablespoon butter.

Bake for 45 minutes. Let it cool for 10 minutes before cutting. Serve warm.

Vegetable and Cheese Burritos

(Ready in about 30 minutes | Servings 2)

Ingredients

2 flour tortillas

1 tablespoon olive oil

1 onion, finely chopped

1 green bell pepper, diced

2 cloves garlic, minced

1 jalapeño chili pepper

1 (15 ounce) can brown beans, rinsed and drained

1/4 cup cooked corn kernels

1/2 soft cheese of choice, crumbled

1/2 teaspoon salt

1/4 teaspoon black pepper

Parsley for garnish, roughly chopped

Directions

Preheat oven to 350 degrees F. Prepare a baking tray.

Wrap tortillas in a foil and transfer them to the baking tray. Bake for about 15 minutes.

Heat olive oil in a medium saucepan over medium-high heat. Sauté the onion until fragrant. Add bell pepper, garlic and jalapenos, and stir-fry for 3 minutes.

Pour beans and corn into the saucepan, and cook 5 minutes, stirring often.

Add the cheese. Cook for 2 minutes more. Season with salt and pepper.

Spoon mixture on tortillas and roll them up. Sprinkle parsley and serve warm.

Spiced Vegetable Patties

(Ready in about 35 minutes | Servings 4)

Ingredients

- 2 cups zucchini,
- 2 eggs
- 1 white onion, chopped
- 1/2 cup all-purpose flour
- 1 mozzarella cheese, shredded
- 1 teaspoon salt
- 1/2 teaspoon black pepper
- 1/2 teaspoon cayenne pepper
- 3 tablespoons vegetable oil
- 1 tablespoon fresh parsley

Directions

To prepare ingredients: Grate the zucchini, chop the onions and shred the chesse. Beat the eggs well.

Combine the zucchini, eggs, onion, flour, mozzarella cheese, salt, black pepper and cayenne pepper. Mix well to combine all ingredients.

Heat oil in a wide saucepan over medium-high heat. Spoon zucchini mixture, place in the saucepan and cook for 5 minutes until golden. Gently flip and cook on the other side for 4 to 5 minutes.

Transfer the cooked patties to serving platter, sprinkle the parsley and serve immediately.

Mediterranean Ratatouille

(Ready in about 1 hour | Servings 4)

Ingredients

2 tablespoons vegetable oil

1 onion, sliced

3 cloves garlic, minced

2 teaspoons dried basil

1 teaspoon salt

1/2 teaspoon freshly ground black pepper

1 eggplant, cut into bite-sized cubes

1 cup Parmesan cheese, shredded

2 zucchini, sliced

2 cups button mushrooms, sliced

2 medium tomatoes, chopped

Fresh parsley, for garnish

Directions

Preheat oven to 350 degrees F. Oil casserole dish with 1 tablespoon of vegetable oil.

Heat remaining 1 tablespoon oil in a medium cast-iron skillet over medium-high flame. Add onion and garlic and sauté until the onion is tender and fragrant.

Stir in basil and eggplant cubes. Cook until the eggplant cubes are soft. Season with salt and pepper.

Spread eggplant mixture evenly on oiled casserole dish. Sprinkle 1/3 cup Parmesan cheese. Layer zucchini and sprinkle 1/3 cup of cheese. Layer mushrooms and tomatoes, and sprinkle remaining 1/3 cup shredded cheese.

Bake for 45 minutes. Sprinkle chopped parsley and let it cool for 10 minutes before serving.

Mexican Chalupas

(Ready in about 40 minutes | Servings 4)

Ingredients

3 ripe avocados

2 tablespoons lime juice

1 tablespoon yoghurt

2 tablespoons fat-free mayonnaise

1 teaspoon fine sea salt

1/2 teaspoon freshly ground pepper

8 wheat tortillas

3 tablespoons canola oil

4 jalapeño peppers, finaly chopped

3 cups semi-hard cheese, shredded

Directions

Peel the avocados, cut them vertically and discard the pits.

To make avocado purée: Place the avocado flesh in a bowl and mix with lime juice, yoghurt, salt, and pepper. Cover and keep in a refrigerator.

Preheat the broiler.

Brush the tortillas with the oil and place them on a baking sheet. Bake until golden.

To make chalupa: Place minced jalapeño peppers on each tortilla. Then layer grated cheese, and broil briefly, or until the cheese is melted. Spread avocado purée among tortillas and serve warm.

Avocado Sandwiches with Eggs

(Ready in about 15 minutes | Servings 4)

Ingredients

8 slices whole-grain bread

2 tablespoons mayonnaise

2 teaspoons Dijon mustard

8 leaves romaine lettuce

1 large tomato, sliced

1 peeled avocado, sliced

4 slices Swiss cheese

2 boiled eggs, sliced

Salt to taste

Black pepper to taste

Directions

Toast the bread slices. Spread mayonnaise and mustard on the slices of bread.

Layer lettuce, tomato, avocado, cheese and eggs on each bread slice. Season with salt and pepper to taste.

Top with remaining bread slices and serve immediately.

Bean and Cheese Tostadas

(Ready in about 45 minutes | Servings 4)

Ingredients

4 tablespoons olive oil

2 white onions, chopped

2 cloves garlic, minced

3 cups black beans

1 cup water

1 teaspoon salt

1/4 teaspoon black pepper

1/2 teaspoon chili powder

8 wheat tortillas

3 cups grated cheese of choice

1/2 cup sour cream

Salsa to taste

Directions

Heat 2 tablespoons of the oil in a wide and deep saucepan over medium-high flame. Add the onions and garlic. Sauté until the onions are tender and translucent, for 10 minutes.

Drain and rinse the black beans under cold water. Add the beans and water to the saucepan, and simmer for 5 minutes. Season with salt and pepper and add chili powder.

Divide the beans in halves. Mash a half of beans and set aside.

Preheat s broiler. Brush the tortillas with 2 remaining tablespoons of oil. Place them on a baking sheet and bake until the tortillas are lightly golden.

Spread a mashed beans on each tortilla equally. Top with grated cheese. Return the tortillas to the broiler and bake until the cheese is melted.

Divide sour cream among tortillas. Serve with salsa and additional sour cream if desired.

Noodles and Cauliflower Stir-Fry

(Ready in about 25 minutes | Servings 4)

Ingredients

2 cups cauliflower, broken into florets

4 tablespoons vegetable oil

1/2 pound firm tofu

2 onions, sliced

3 cloves garlic, minced

3 cups cooked noodles

2 tablespoons soy sauce

2 tablespoons sesame oil

Directions

In a medium pot, cook the cauliflower with 1/4 cup water over medium heat. Cook the cauliflower until soft. Reserve.

Heat the oil in a wide saucepan over medium-high heat. Cut the tofu into bite-sized cubes and pat dry. Add the tofu to the hot oil and cook until golden.

Add the onions and garlic and sauté for 5 minutes, stirring frequently, until the onions are tender and translucent. Add the cauliflower florets and toss. Cook for 2 minutes more.

Add the cooked noodles and toss. Add the soy sauce and stir-fry for 2 minutes longer.

Drizzle the sesame oil and serve at room temperature.

Mushroom Cheeseburgers

(Ready in about 35 minutes | Servings 4)

Ingredients

4 large mushrooms of choice

2 tablespoons apple cider vinegar

2 tablespoons olive oil

1 teaspoon dried rosemary

1 teaspoon dried oregano

2 cloves garlic, minced

1 teaspoon salt

1/4 teaspoon black pepper

1/4 teaspoon red pepper flakes

4 slices hard cheese

4 burger-style buns

baby gem lettuce leaves, for garnish

Directions

Whisk vinegar, oil, rosemary, oregano, garlic, salt, black pepper and red pepper flakes in a medium bowl. Mix well to combine all ingredients. Pour the mixture over the mushrooms. Let stand to marinate for about 30 minutes.

Preheat grill to medium heat and brush it with olive oil.

Place mushrooms on the grill. Grill for 8 minutes until soft and heated through. Drizzle the marinade often. Top with cheese slices before the end of baking.

Divide the mushroom burgers among 4 buns, add baby gem lettuce and serve immediately.

Curry Vegetables with Tofu and Coconut

(Ready in about 40 minutes | Servings 6)

Ingredients

- 1 (14 ounce) can light coconut milk
- 1/4 cup soy sauce, divided
- 1 teaspoon curry powder
- 2 teaspoons chile paste
- 1 pound firm tofu
- 4 medium tomatoes, sliced
- 1 red bell pepper, thinly sliced
- 4 ounces fresh mushrooms, chopped
- 2 bunches scallions
- 1/4 cup fresh basil, chopped
- 4 cups bok choy, chopped
- 1 teaspoon kosher salt
- 1/2 teaspoon freshly ground black pepper

Directions

Heat a deep and wide saucepan over medium-high heat. Whisk coconut milk, soy sauce, curry powder, and chile paste. Add the mixture in the saucepan and bring to a boil.

Cut the tofu into small cubes. Stir tofu, tomatoes, pepper, mushrooms, and chopped scallions into the saucepan. Cover, and cook 5 minutes, stirring often.

Add basil, bok choy, salt and black pepper. Cook for another 5 minutes, or until vegetables are just tender. Serve warm.

Macaroni Like Grandma Used to Make

(Ready in about 1 hour | Servings 6)

Ingredients

- 2 tablespoons vegetable oil
- 1/4 cup onion, chopped
- 2 tablespoons all-purpose flour
- 2 cups milk
- 1 teaspoon salt
- 1/4 teaspoon ground black pepper
- 1 teaspoon dried oregano
- 1 teaspoon dried basil
- 1 (8 ounce) package macaroni
- 2 cups Cheddar cheese, shredded
- 1 (8 ounce) package processed firm cheese, cut into strip

Directions

Preheat oven to 350 degrees F. Butter a baking dish.

Heat the oil in a wide skillet over medium-high heat. Sauté the onion until tender and translucent Mix in flour and cook 1 minute, stirring often.

Add milk, salt, pepper, oregano and basil, and continue cooking, stirring frequently, until mixture is thickened.

To prepare macaroni: Bring a pot of salted water to a boil. Add macaroni and cook for 10 to 12 minutes. Drain, rinse nad set aside.

Add the cheese to prepared milk and spices mixture and cook until cheese is melted. Mix macaroni and milk-cheese sauce and mix well to combine ingredients. Transfer to the baking dish.

Bake in the middle of the oven for 30 minutes, or until golden. Let stand for 10 minutes and serve warm.

Hot Tomato and Cheese Sandwiches

(Ready in about 15 minutes | Servings 2)

Ingredients

2 medium tomatoes, sliced

2 tablespoons extra-virgin olive oil

1 teaspoon kosher salt

3 tablespoons mayonnaise

1 teaspoon dried basil

1/4 teaspoon dried oregano

1/4 teaspoon black pepper

3 tablespoons Parmesan cheese, shredded

4 slices bread of choice

6 black olives, pitted and sliced

Directions

Set the oven to broil. Prepare a baking sheet.

Drizzle olive oil over tomato slices and season them with salt.

Combine mayonnaise, basil, oregano and black pepper in a medium mixing bowl.

Spread mayonnaise and spices mixture on each slice of bread. Layer oiled tomatoes and then layer shredded Parmesan cheese. Top with sliced olives.

Place on the prepared baking sheet and broil for 5 minutes, or until cheese is melted. Serve warm.

Breaded Cheese Ravioli

(Ready in about 30 minutes | Servings 4)

Ingredients

2 tablespoons whole milk

2 egg

1 cup bread crumbs

1 teaspoon salt

1 cup tomato sauce

1 package frozen cheese ravioli, thawed

cooking oil for deep-frying

Directions

Whisk milk and eggs in a bowl. Season with salt. Dip cheese ravioli in the mixture, and coat with bread crumbs.

Heat a wide and deep saucepan over medium flame and cook tomato sauce for 10 minutes, until heated through. Cover and set aside.

Heat cooking oil over medium-high heat. Fry breaded cheese ravioli, on each side, until golden brown. Serve warm with hot tomato sauce.

Potato Salad with Spinach

(Ready in about 20 minutes | Servings 4)

Ingredients

16 oz. baby red potatoes, diced

8 oz. green beans

6 tablespoons canola oil

6 scallions, chopped

4 tablespoons apple cider vinegar

2 tablespoons chopped fresh parsley

1/2 teaspoon black pepper

1 teaspoon salt

8 cups baby spinach leaves

Directions

Bring a pot of salted water to a boil. Boil potatoes until soft. Add green beans and cook briefly, for 5 minutes more.

Heat canola oil in a cast-iron skillet over medium-high heat. Sauté the scallions for about 4 minutes. Remove from heat and add apple cider vinegar.

Drain potatoes and green beans. Toss with scallion and vinegar mixture, then add parsley and black pepper. Season with salt, taste, and adjust the seasonings. Serve warm with spinach leaves.

Bean Tostadas with Greens and Salsa

(Ready in about 30 minutes | Servings 4)

Ingredients

4 whole-wheat tortillas

2 tablespoons olive oil

1 onion, finely chopped

1 (15-ounces) can brown beans

1 teaspoon cayenne pepper

1/2 teaspoon dried basil

4 cloves garlic, minced

2 ½ cups kale, cut into strips

1 teaspoon salt

1/4 teaspoon black pepper

1 cup prepared chipotle salsa

2 tablespoons cilantro, chopped

2 tablespoons sour cream

2 tablespoons mayonnaise of choice

Directions

Preheat oven to 425 degrees F. Brush both sides of tortillas with oil. Bake on a baking sheet for 10 minutes.

Heat 1 tablespoon olive oil in a wide skillet over medium-high heat. Add the onion to hot oil, and sauté until soft and translucent. Drain and rinse beans, and add them to the skillet. Add cayenne and basil, reduce heat to medium and cook for 10 minutes more.

Heat remaining 1 tablespoon oil in the skillet over medium heat. Add garlic and cook 2 minutes, until fragrant.

Stir in kale strips, and season with salt and pepper. Cook for about 5 minutes.

Divide bean mixture among prepared tortillas. Top with greens and salsa. Sprinkle cilantro and serve with sour cream and mayonnaise.

Curried Tempeh Tacos

(Ready in about 25 minutes | Servings 4)

Ingredients

2 tablespoons olive oil

1 onion, chopped

1 (8-ounces) package tempeh, cut into bite-sized cubes

2 tablespoons cilantro, chopped

2 teaspoon curry powder

1 teaspoon fresh ginger, minced

1 teaspoon salt

1/4 teaspoon black pepper

2 tablespoons lemon juice

4 flour tortillas, warmed

2 red bell peppers, thinly sliced

2 tablespoons chopped walnuts

Directions

Heat oil in a caste-iron skillet over medium-high heat. Add onion, and sauté for 5 minutes, or until tender and translucent.

Stir in tempeh, cilantro, curry powder, and ginger. Season with salt and pepper. Cook 5 minutes, stirring often, until tempeh begins to brown. Remove from the heat and stir in lemon juice.

Fill tortillas with prepared tempeh mixture. Add red slices of bell pepper. Taste and adjust the seasonings.

Top with walnuts and serve immediately.

Spiced Vegetable Pizza

(Ready in about 25 minutes | Servings 4)

Ingredients

1 pound whole-wheat pizza dough
2 tablespoons oil
1 garlic clove, minced
3 ripe tomatoes, sliced
5 medium mushrooms of choice, sliced
1/2 teaspoon dried oregano
1/2 teaspoon dried basil
1/2 teaspoon salt
1/2 cup Mozzarella, shredded
Ketchup for garnish (optional)
Sour cream for garnish (optional)

Directions

Preheat oven to 500 degrees F. Set a rack on the lowest position. Line a baking sheet with parchment paper.

Roll dough into a round shape on a floured surface. Transfer the dough on the baking sheet.

Combine oil and garlic and brush on dough. Then layer tomato and sliced mushrooms. Sprinkle the oregano, basil and salt. Top with Mozzarella cheese.

Bake until the crust is golden and crisp, for about 15 minutes. Let stand for 5 minutes before cutting and serving. Serve with ketchup and sour cream.

Smoked Cheese and Zucchini Pizza

(Ready in about 25 minutes | Servings 4)

Ingredients

1 pound whole-wheat pizza dough
2 tablespoon olive oil
4 green onions, sliced
2 small zucchini, thinly sliced
1/4 teaspoon salt
1/4 teaspoon black pepper
1/4 teaspoon smoked paprika
3/4 ounce smoked Parmesan, grated
2 tablespoons fresh rosemary
1 teaspoon oregano
1 teaspoon basil

Directions

Preheat oven to 500 degrees F. Line a baking sheet with parchment paper.

On a floured surface, roll out and stretch pizza dough into desired shape. Place the dough on the baking sheet.

Drizzle oil and scatter onions on the dough. Layer zucchini and season with salt and pepper. Sprinkle smoked paprika, rosemary, oregano and basil. Top with Parmesan.

Bake until crust is crisp and cheese is melted. Let the pizza rest for several minutes before cutting and serving.

PART FOUR FAST SNACKS

Quick Guacamole with Sour Cream

(Ready in about 45 minutes | Servings 4)

Ingredients

2 avocados

1 red onion, finely chopped

1 clove garlic, minced

1 ripe tomato, chopped

Juice from 1 lemon

1 teaspoon salt

1/4 teaspoon freshly ground black pepper

4 tablespoons sour cream

Directions

Peel and mash avocados in a large bowl.

Mix in onion, garlic, tomato, lemon juice, salt and pepper. Taste and adjust the seasonings.

Garnish with sour cream and serve chilled with tortilla chips.

Carrot and Zucchini Wraps

(Ready in about 50 minutes | Servings 4)

Ingredients

3 green onions, sliced

3 garlic cloves, minced

2 large carrots, shredded

4 zucchini, shredded

4 tablespoons flour

2 tablespoons lemon juice

1 tablespoon fresh coriander, roughly chopped

1 teaspoon salt

1/4 teaspoon black pepper

16 spring roll wrappers

Cooking oil for deep-frying

Sour dipping sauce for garnish

Directions

To make a filling: Heat a little oil in a wide cast-iron skillet. Sauté the onions and garlic until tender. Add the shredded carrots and zucchini and cook until crisp-soft.

Sprinkle the flour and cook for 5 minutes.

Remove the skillet from the stove and add the lemon juice and coriander. Season with salt and pepper. Set aside to cool slightly.

To make the parcels: Place the spring roll wrappers and cover them with a tea towel. Divide prepared filling among 16 roll wrappers. Roll the wrappers over until they resemble a small cylinders.

Continue until all the wrappers have been used.

Heat oil in the skillet in order to deep-fry the wraps. Fry the wraps until they are golden and crisp.

Replace the fried wraps on paper towel to soak excess oil. Transfer prepared wraps onto a serving platter and serve with your favorite sour dipping sauce.

Chickpea Chili Bites

(Ready in about 45 minutes | Servings 6)

Ingredients

1 ½ cup chickpeas, canned

1/2 cup self-raising flour

1/2 cup chickpea flour

1 teaspoon baking powder

1 teaspoon ground ginger

1 teaspoon cayenne pepper

1 medium onion, finely chopped

2 chilies, seeded and minced

2 cups spinach, uncooked and chopped

1/2 teaspoon salt

1/4 teaspoon black pepper

1 cup water

cooking oil for deep-frying

mayonnaise and ketchup for garnish

Directions

Drain and rinse the chickpeas. Place the chickpeas in a mixing bowl and mash them. Add the flours, baking powder, ginger, cayenne pepper, onion, chilies and spinach.

Season with salt and black pepper. Stir to combine all ingredients. Add the water and stir again.

Heat the cooking oil in a wide and deep saucepan. Drop spoonful of the chickpea mash into the hot oil. Continue until all the chickpea mash has been used.

Deep-fry until bites are golden and crisp. Remove to a paper towel and drain them.

Transfer to a serving platter and serve with mayonnaise and ketchup.

Toasted Rye Bread with Creamy Mushrooms

(Ready in about 25 minutes | Servings 4)

Ingredients

2 tablespoons olive oil

3 green onions, sliced

3 garlic cloves, minced

1 cup dry white wine

1 cup Heavy Whipping Cream

2 cups mushrooms, sliced

4 slices of rye bread

1 teaspoon salt

1/2 teaspoon milled black pepper

Red pepper flakes for garnish

Directions

Heat the oil in a large heavy skillet over medium-high heat. Sauté the onions and garlic for 5 minutes. Then add a wine in the skillet, and cook, stirring often, until the liquid is almost absorbed.

Reduce the heat to medium-low, then stir in the heavy cream. Add the mushrooms and cook for 5 minutes or until the mushrooms are tender and fragrant. Season with salt and pepper.

Meanwhile, place slices of rye bread under a heated grill and toast them.

Taste the mushroom mixture and adjust the seasonings.

Spoon the mushroom mixture onto the toasted rye slices. Sprinkle red pepper flakes on top and serve.

Garlicky and Creamy Stuffed Mushrooms

(Ready in about 45 minutes | Servings 6)

Ingredients

2 tablespoon extra-virgin olive oil

12 large mushrooms

1 tablespoon garlic, minced

1 cup semi-soft cheese, shredded

1 teaspoon garlic salt

1/2 teaspoon freshly ground black pepper

1/4 teaspoon smoked paprika

1 teaspoon basil

Fresh parsley for garnish

Directions

Preheat oven to 350 degrees F. Lightly oil a baking sheet.

Gently break off stems from the mushrooms. Chop stems and set aside.

Heat oil in a deep and wide saucepan or wok over medium-high heat. Add chopped mushroom stems and garlic in a hot oil. Cook for 10 minutes, or until all liquid is absorbed. Set aside to cool.

To make the filling: Add the cheese into chilled mushroom mixture. Season with garlic salt, black pepper, smoked paprika and basil.

Fill mushrooms by using a spoon.

Place the mushroom caps on prepared baking sheet. Bake for 20 minutes. Transfer to a serving platter, sprinkle parsley and serve.

Garlic-Parmesan Bread with Tomato Dip

(Ready in about 30 minutes | Servings 8)

Ingredients

1/2 cup butter, melted

1 teaspoon salt

1/4 teaspoon black pepper

1/4 teaspoon dried basil

1/4 teaspoon tarragon

1/4 teaspoon garlic powder

1 tablespoon Parmesan cheese, shredded

1 loaf Italian-style baguette

Tomato Dip or ketchup for garnish

Directions

Preheat oven to 300 degrees F. Prepare a cookie sheet.

Stir in the butter, salt, black pepper, basil, tarragon, garlic powder and Parmesan cheese.

Cut baguette into very thin slices. Spread each slice of bread with prepared garlic and cheese mixture.

Place bread slices onto prepared cookie sheet. Bake for 10 to 12 minutes, or until the edges of bread slices become golden brown.

Transfer to a serving tray and serve with Tomato Dip or ketchup.

Homemade Tortilla Chips with Salsa

(Ready in about 25 minutes | Servings 6)

Ingredients

1 (12-ounce) package corn tortillas

2 tablespoons olive oil

Juice from 1 fresh lemon

1 teaspoon chili powder

1 teaspoon salt

1 teaspoon red pepper flakes

1 teaspoon paprika

Salsa sauce for garnish

Directions

Preheat oven to 350 degrees F. Line a baking sheet with parchment paper.

Slice the tortillas into bite-sized wedges. Mix the oil and lemon juice.

Place the tortilla wedges on the baking sheet. Drizzle with oil and lemon mixture. Sprinkle chili powder, salt, red pepper and paprika.

Bake for 15 minutes, or until chips are golden and crisp. Remove from the oven and serve with your favorite salsa.

Lentil Spread with Slipper Bread

(Ready in about 20 minutes | Servings 4)

Ingredients

- 2 tablespoons canola oil
- 2 red onions, chopped
- 2 garlic cloves, minced
- 2 cups brown lentils, cooked
- 1 teaspoon thyme
- 1 teaspoon rosemary
- 1 tablespoon Worcestershire sauce
- 3 tablespoons water
- 1 teaspoon garlic salt
- 1/2 teaspoon freshly ground black pepper
- toasted ciabatta (slipper bread)

Directions

Heat canola oil in a wide and deep skillet. Sauté the onions and garlic until tender.

Add the cooked lentils, and cook for 5 minutes. Add the thyme, rosemary, Worcestershire sauce, water, salt and pepper and stir well.

Cook over medium heat for about 10 minutes. Taste and adjust the seasonings. Spread lentil mixture onto lightly toasted slipper bread. Serve at room temperature.

Mini Pita with Greek Dip

(Ready in about 1 hour 15 minutes | Servings 6)

Ingredients

- 1/2 cucumber
- 1 cup whole yogurt
- 1 tablespoon extra-virgin olive oil
- 2 cloves garlic, minced
- 1/2 teaspoon garlic powder
- 1 tablespoon fresh dill
- 1/4 teaspoon salt
- whole wheat mini pita for serving

Directions

Peel the cucumber. Grate the cucumber and transfer onto clean kitchen towel.

Squeeze out all the liquid form grated cucumber. Place the cucumber in a serving bowl.

Stir in the yogurt, olive oil, garlic, garlic powder, dill, and salt.

Chill for 1 hour and serve with whole wheat mini pita.

Mini Pita Pockets with Spiced Eggs

(Ready in about 1 hour 25 minutes | Servings 4)

Ingredients

- 1/4 cup mayonnaise
- 1 scallion, sliced
- 1 tablespoon balsamic vinegar
- 1 teaspoon mustard
- 1/2 teaspoon curry powder
- 4 hard-boiled egg, chopped
- 1 apple, peeled and cut into bite-sized cubes
- 1 teaspoon salt
- 1/4 teaspoon ground white pepper
- 8 mini pita pockets
- Black olives for garnish

Directions

Whisk mayonnaise, scallion, balsamic vinegar, mustard, curry powder in a deep mixing bowl. Stir in eggs and apple cubes.

Season with salt and white pepper.

Fill mini pita pockets, garnish with olives and serve at room temperature.

Cheese Herb Spread with Crackers

(Ready in about 15 minutes + chilling | Servings 4)

Ingredients

- 2 cups plain yogurt
- 1 clove garlic, minced
- 1 tablespoon olive oil
- 1/2 teaspoon fresh thyme
- 1 teaspoon minced fresh basil
- 1 teaspoon salt
- 1/4 teaspoon black pepper

Directions

Line a strainer with cheesecloth and place the strainer over a wide and deep bowl. Place the yogurt into the center of the strainer and let sit for 4 to 12 hours in a fridge.

The yogurt-cheese should resemble ricotta cheese.

Place the yogurt cheese in a serving bowl. Stir in garlic, olive oil, thyme, basil, salt and pepper and mix to combine well.

Cover and chill for 2 to 3 hours before serving. Serve as a spread on crackers.

Ricotta Spread with Pepper Strips

(Ready in about 15 minutes + chilling | Servings 6)

Ingredients

1 cup ricotta cheese

1/4 cup semi-hard cheese, shredded

2 tablespoons whole milk

1 clove garlic, minced

1 teaspoon dried basil

2 tablespoons fresh parsley, finely chopped

1 teaspoon kosher salt

1/4 teaspoon black pepper, milled

2 yellow bell peppers

1 green bell pepper

2 red bell peppers

Directions

Whisk Ricotta, shredded cheese, milk, garlic, basil, parsley, salt and black pepper in a bowl until smooth.

Cover the prepared spread and chill for 1 hour before serving. Sprinkle additional parsley.

Slice the peppers into long strips. Serve with chilled ricotta spread.

Brussels Sprout Chips with Cheese

(Ready in about 25 minutes | Servings 4)

Ingredients

20 large Brussels sprouts, trimmed

5 tablespoons olive oil

1/4 teaspoon freshly ground black pepper

1/2 cup Parmesan cheese, shredded

Directions

Preheat oven to 325 degrees F. Line a baking sheet with parchment paper.

Place Brussels sprouts leaves in a wide and deep bowl. Add olive oil and sprinkle salt and pepper. Toss to combine ingredients.

Layer prepared leaves on the baking sheet and bake for about 20 minutes. Remove from the oven. Scatter the Parmesan cheese.

Let stand on a wire rack for 15 minutes and serve.

Pita Bread Triangles with Eggplant Dip

(Ready in about 1 hour 10 minutes | Servings 8)

Ingredients

- 1 medium eggplant
- 3 tablespoons butter
- 2 teaspoons ground coriander
- 1/2 teaspoon turmeric
- 1/8 teaspoon paprika
- 1 clove garlic, minced
- 1/2 cup finely chopped tomato
- 1 tablespoon salt
- 1/4 teaspoon red pepper flakes
- 3 tablespoons yogurt
- Fresh coriander for garnish

Directions

Preheat the oven to 400 degrees F. Lightly grease a baking sheet.

Peel the eggplant. Prick the eggplant with a fork in a few places.

Place the eggplant on the baking sheet. Bake for 1 hour, or until the eggplant is very tender. Let sit until the eggplant is chilled enough to handle. Scoop out the pulp of the eggplant.

Heat the butter in a wide saucepan. Add the coriander, turmeric, paprika, and garlic, and stir-fry for 2 to 3 minutes. Stir in the tomato and cook 2 minutes longer.

Mash eggplant pulp until smooth. Add the spices, tomato mixture and yogurt. Season with salt and red pepper.

Cover and chill overnight.

Replace to a serving bowl and garnish with fresh coriander. Serve with hot pita bread triangles.

Stuffed Mushrooms with Feta and Herbs

(Ready in about 30 minutes | Servings 4)

Ingredients

- 1/2 cup almonds, chopped
- 1/2 cup bread crumbs
- 1 tablespoon rosemary, finely chopped
- 1 tablespoon parsley, chopped
- 3/4 cup feta cheese, crumbled
- 2 tablespoons milk
- 1/4 teaspoon freshly ground black pepper
- 16 large mushrooms
- 3 tablespoons olive oil

Directions

Preheat the oven to 375 degrees F. Grease a baking dish.

To prepare the filling: Combine the almonds, bread crumbs, rosemary, parsley, feta cheese, milk, and pepper together in a deep bowl.

Wipe the mushrooms. Remove the stems and reserve for another use.

Stuff the mushrooms with prepared filling.

Place the mushrooms on the baking dish. Drizzle the oil over mushrooms.

Bake for 20 minutes, or until the mushrooms are lightly browned. Sprinkle parsley if desired and serve warm.

Spiced Corn Crackers

(Ready in about 50 minutes | Servings 8)

Ingredients

1 ¼ cup warm water

2 tablespoons sesame seeds

1 teaspoon salt

2 tablespoons nutritional yeast

1 tablespoon coconut

1/4 cup nuts almonds

1/4 cup walnuts

2 tablespoons sunflower seeds

1/4 teaspoon garlic powder

1 teaspoon onion powder

1 ¼ cup cornmeal

1/2 cup warm water

Directions

Combine 1 ¼ cup water, sesame seeds, salt, nutritional yeast, coconut, almonds, walnuts, sunflower seeds, garlic powder and onion powder. Process this mixture in an electric blender or a food processor until smooth.

Preheat oven to 350 degrees F.

Combine blended mixture with cornmeal and 1/2 cup warm water.

Butter a baking sheet. Spread the batter to the baking sheet and poke fork holes. Cut the batter into crackers with cookie cutter.

Bake for 30 minutes or until the crackers are golden brown.

Apple Pecan Popcorn

(Ready in about 55 minutes | Servings 6)

Ingredients

2 cups dried apples, chopped

10 cups popped popcorn

2 cups pecan halves

4 tablespoons butter, melted

1 teaspoon allspice

3 tablespoons brown sugar

Directions

Preheat oven to 250 degrees F.

Place dried apples in a large baking sheet and bake for 20 minutes.

Combine together popcorn and pecans. Mix the butter, allspice and brown sugar and stir to combine ingredients.

Drizzle spiced butter mixture over popcorn and nuts mixture.

Bake for 30 minutes, stirring occasionally. Combine with baked apples and serve.

Baked Mushrooms with Cheese and Eggs

(Ready in about 40 minutes | Servings 4)

Ingredients

2 tablespoons raw sunflower seeds

12 large mushrooms

1/3 cup blue cheese, crumbled

1/4 cup soft cheese

2 tablespoons milk

2 tablespoons fine cracker crumbs

2 tablespoons fresh parsley

2 boiled eggs, crumbled

Directions

Preheat the oven to 400 degrees F.

Remove the stems from the mushrooms. Finely chop the stems.

Place the sunflower seeds in a large baking tray in the middle of the oven. Toast them until they are golden, or for 8 minutes.

Mash the blue cheese, soft cheese, and milk until smooth. Mix in the sunflower seeds, chopped stems and cracker crumbs.

Fill the mushrooms cap with this mixture. Place the mushrooms onto the oiled baking dish.

Bake for 20 minutes, or until the mushrooms are fragrant and juicy. Transfer to a serving tray, scatter the eggs and top with parsley. Serve warm.

Pecan Popcorn with Delicious Syrup

(Ready in about 30 minutes | Servings 8)

Ingredients

8 cups popped popcorn

Non-stick spray coating

1/2 cups pecans

3 tablespoons butter, melted

1/3 cup corn syrup

1/4 cup instant butter pecan pudding mix

1/2 teaspoon cinnamon

Directions

Preheat the oven to 300 degrees F. Spray a baking pan with non-stick coating.

Place the popped corn and pecans in the baking pan.

To make the syrup mixture: Heat the butter in a skillet. Add corn syrup, pudding mix and cinnamon.

Pour hot syrup over popcorn and toss to combine well.

Bake popcorn for 15 minutes, stirring occasionally.

When the popcorn chilled, break it into pieces. Store covered popcorn in a cool and dry place for 1 week.

Red Quinoa and Avocado Appetizer

(Ready in about 20 minutes | Servings 8)

Ingredients

1/3 cup red quinoa

1/2 teaspoon chili powder

1 cup water

Juice from one fresh lemon

1 tablespoon orange zest

2 tablespoons extra-virgin olive oil

1/2 teaspoon salt

1/4 teaspoon black pepper

1/2 teaspoon dried basil

1 ripe avocado

1/3 cup alfalfa sprouts

Directions

Place quinoa, chili powder and 1 cup water to a deep saucepan, and bring to a boil, over medium-high heat.

Cover, lower heat, and simmer 15 minutes, or until the most water is evaporated.

Mix together lemon juice and olive oil. Add cooked quinoa and toss to coat. Season with salt, pepper and basil.

Slice avocado into small bite-sized cubes.

Divide quinoa among 8 portions. Add avocado cubes and top with alfalfa sprouts. Serve immediately.

Stuffed Peppadews Bites

(Ready in about 10 minutes | Servings 6)

Ingredients

12 fresh mint leaves

12 Peppadews

1 small cucumber

2 tablespoons semi-soft cheese, crumbled

1 tablespoon sweet paprika

6 sage leaves to garnish

Directions

Rinse and drain Peppadews. Peel cucumber, discard the seeds and slice into very small chunks.

To make the filling: Combine toogether mint leaves, cucumber and semi-soft cheese.

Stuff the Peppadews. Sprinkle sweet paprika and place sage leaves on top.

Serve chilled.

Party Potato Cakes

(Ready in about 15 minutes | Servings 4)

Ingredients

2 cups new potatoes, cooked

1 egg

1 tablespoon flour

2 tablespoons whole milk

Salt to taste

Black pepper to taste

1/4 cup canola oil

Fresh parsley, roughly chopped

Directions

Peel cooked potatoes and mash with a potato masher. Mix mashed potatoes, egg, flour, and milk. Season with salt and pepper.

Stir to combine all ingredients well. Form potato mixture into flat cakes.

Heat canola oil in a cast-iron skillet. Place cakes in a hot oil and fry until golden brown.

Transfer to a paper towel to soak excess oil. Place to a serving platter, sprinkle the parsley and serve immediately.

Garbanzo Bean-Cumin Dip with Corn Crackers

(Ready in about 15 minutes | Servings 4)

Ingredients

- 1 (15-ounce) can Garbanzo beans, drained
- 2 tablespoons extra-virgin olive oil
- 1 tablespoon balsamic vinegar
- 1 small red onion, finely chopped
- 1 teaspoon salt
- 1/4 teaspoon black pepper, milled
- 1/2 teaspoon paprika
- 1 teaspoon ground cumin
- Corn crackers of choice, for garnish

Directions

To make purée: Mash garbanzo beans in a mixing bowl until smooth.

Add oil, balsamic vinegar and chopped red onions and mix to combine.

Season with salt, pepper and paprika. Add cumin and mix well.

Serve with your favorite crackers.

Tarator Sauce with Fried Vegetables

(Ready in about 15 minutes + chilling | Servings 6)

Ingredients

- 2 cucumbers, peeled and chopped
- 1 garlic clove, minced
- 4 cups yoghurt
- 1/2 cup water
- 1/4 teaspoon salt
- 2 tablespoons dill, chopped
- toasted walnuts for garnishing, chopped

Directions

Process cucumber and garlic in an electric blender or food processor.

Stir in the yogurt, water, salt and dill and pulse until they become frothy.

Refrigerate for 2 hours or overnight.

Divide chilled Tarator among a few serving bowls, sprinkle with toasted walnuts and serve with fried vegetables (e.g. fried cauliflower).

Party Baby Reubens

(Ready in about 25 minutes | Servings 12)

Ingredients

- 40 slices of party rye bread
- 2 tablespoons olive oil
- 2 packages (6-ounces) baby portobello mushrooms, sliced
- 2 teaspoons Dijon mustard
- 1 cup shredded Swiss cheese
- 1 (10-ounces) can sauerkraut, rinsed

Directions

Place rye bread slices on a baking sheet and broil for 2 minutes.

Heat the oil in a medium skillet and sauté the mushroom for 10 minutes, or until they are soft and fragrant.

Remove the bread slices from oven. Spread mustard over the slices of bread. Layer mushrooms, cheese and sauerkraut on each slice of bread.

Broil for 5 minutes more. Arrange to a serving platter and serve warm.

Pecans and Cashews Snack Mix

(Ready in about 1 hour 10 minutes | Servings 12)

Ingredients

- 1/2 cup butter
- 3/4 cup corn syrup
- 1 cup brown sugar
- 1 cup pecans, chopped
- 1 cup cashews, chopped
- 1 (12-ounce) package corn and rice cereal

Directions

Preheat oven to 275 degrees F. Oil a baking pan with non-stick cooking spray.

Combine together butter, white corn syrup, and brown sugar.

Place the mixture in the microwave and cook 2 minutes. Place the pecans, cashews and cereal into the oiled baking pan.

Add the melted butter mixture to the cereal mixture and mix to combine. Bake for 1 hour, stirring occasionally. Chill the snacks and serve.

Cheese Mini Bruschetta

(Ready in about 25 minutes | Servings 8)

Ingredients

1/2 cup mayonnaise

1 cup mozzarella cheese, shredded

2 ripe tomatoes, chopped

1/4 cup olives, pitted and chopped

1/4 cup parmesan cheese, shredded

1 teaspoon basil

1 teaspoon black pepper

1 baguette

1/3 cup butter, melted

Dried rosemary for garnish

Directions

Preheat oven to 350 degrees F. Prepare a baking sheet.

Combine mayonnaise, mozzarella, tomatoes, olives, Parmesan, basil and black pepper.

Cut the baguette into thin slices. Butter each slice of bread just on one side. Place the slices of baguette on the baking sheet.

Spread the mixture on prepared bread slices. Bake for 15 minutes or until the cheese is melted. Sprinkle rosemary and serve immediately.

Fig-Almonds and Cheese Canapés

(Ready in about 25 minutes | Servings 8)

Ingredients

1 cup dried figs, chopped

1 cup water

1 tablespoon grapeseed oil

2 tablespoons apple cider vinegar

1 teaspoon fresh thyme, chopped

1/4 teaspoon sweet paprika

1/2 cup black olives, pitted and chopped

2 cloves garlic, minced

1 teaspoon kosher salt

1/4 teaspoon ground black pepper

5 tablespoons chopped toasted almonds

1 cup cream cheese

French-style baguette

Directions

Place chopped figs and water in a wide and deep saucepan over medium-high heat. Bring to a boil and cook until the figs are tender and water is almost absorbed.

Turn off heat and stir in oil, vinegar, thyme, and paprika. Add olives and garlic and stir well. Season with salt and pepper.

Cover, and refrigerate at least 4 hours.

Prepare your favorite slices of French-style baguette. Spread the cheese over each slice, then layer fig-almonds spread and top with toasted almonds.

Mini Fruit and Cinnamon Triangles

(Ready in about 20 minutes + chilling | Servings 10)

Ingredients

1 kiwi, peeled and diced

1 medium orange, peeled and diced

2 apples, cored and diced

1 (8-ounce) package raspberries

1 pound strawberries

3 tablespoons brown sugar

3 tablespoons fruit preserves

10 flour tortillas

butter for baking

1 cup cinnamon sugar

Directions

Preheat oven to 350 degrees F. Lightly grease a baking pan.

Combine together kiwi, orange, apples, raspberries, strawberries, sugar and fruit preserves.

Chill the fruit mixture in the refrigerator for 30 minutes. Butter one side of each flour tortilla. Cut the tortillas into small triangles and place on the baking pan.

Sprinkle tortillas with cinnamon sugar. Bake for 10 minutes.

Chill the prepared tortillas at least 15 minutes before serving.

Honey-Roasted Peanuts Spread

(Ready in about 1 hour 10 minutes | Servings 8)

Ingredients

2 tablespoons orange juice

1 tablespoon honey

1 (8-ounces) package cream cheese

1/2 cup raisins

1/4 cup chopped honey-roasted peanuts

Directions

Process orange juice, honey and cream cheese in an electric blender or a food processor.

Stir in raisins and peanuts and mix to combine all ingredients.

Chill for 1 hour before serving. Serve with your favorite crackers.

Tortilla Chips with Hot Spinach Dip

(Ready in about 25 minutes | Servings 12)

Ingredients

1 (16-ounce) jar salsa

1 (10-ounce) package spinach, chopped

2 cups semi-hard cheese, shredded

1 (8-ounce) package soft cheese

1 cup evaporated milk

1/2 cup olives, pitted and chopped

1 tablespoon balsamic vinegar

1 teaspoon fine sea salt

1/4 teaspoon freshly ground black pepper

Tortilla chips of choice

Directions

Preheat oven to 400 degrees F.

Combine together salsa, spinach, semi-hard cheese, soft cheese, milk, olives, vinegar, salt, and pepper. Stir well to combine ingredients.

Bake prepared spinach-cheese mixture for 15 minutes, or until the mixture is bubbly.

Serve at room temperature with your favorite tortilla chips.

Garlicky Breadsticks with Tomato Sauce

(Ready in about 1 hour 20 minutes | Servings 12)

Ingredients

1 bread dough

Non-stick cooking oil spray

2 teaspoons garlic powder

1 teaspoon dried basil

1 teaspoon salt

1/2 cup olive oil

1 small onion, finely chopped

2 cloves garlic, chopped

1/2 teaspoon garlic salt

1/4 teaspoon freshly ground black pepper

1 (32-ounce) can crushed tomatoes

basil leaves to taste

Directions

Preheat oven to 350 degrees F. Oil a baking sheet.

Oil your fingers and knead the dough. Stir in garlic powder, basil, and salt and knead again.

Then shape and divide the dough into small cigar-sized pieces.

Let rise in a warm place until the dough is doubled or for 1 hour. Spray the breadsticks with oil, and bake for 20 minutes. Transfer to a wire rack and let it cool.

Meanwhile, prepare homemade tomato sauce. Heat oil in a wide saucepan over medium heat. Sauté onion and garlic until the onion is translucent, about 3 minutes. Season with garlic salt and pepper.

Add tomatoes and basil, cover and simmer until the sauce is thick enough.

Serve chilled breadsticks with prepared tomato sauce.

Teatime Parmesan Popovers

(Ready in about 1 hour | Servings 9)

Ingredients

3 eggs

1 cup milk

3 tablespoons melted butter

1 cup flour

1/2 teaspoon salt

1/4 cup parmesan cheese, shredded

Directions

Preheat oven to 375 degrees F. Butter a cupcake pan.

Beat eggs with a hand mixer. Stir in milk and melted butter. Gradually add the flour and salt.

Spoon parmesan in each muffin cup.

Pour muffin batter in cups evenly.

Bake popovers 40 minutes or until they are brown and crisp. Serve warm.

Basic Glazed Onions

(Ready in about 15 minutes | Servings 4)

Ingredients

2 tablespoons butter, unsalted

1 package (16-ounces) frozen whole onions, thawed

2 tablespoons brown sugar

1 tablespoons Dijon mustard

2 tablespoons fresh basil, minced

Directions

Melt the butter in a wide and deep saucepan over medium-high heat. Sauté the onions, stirring occasionally, until the onions are brown, or for 12 minutes.

Stir in the brown sugar and Dijon mustard and mix to combine. Cook until the sauce is smooth

Sprinkle with basil and serve immediately.

Stuffed Okra Fingers

(Ready in about 30 minutes | Servings 6)

Ingredients

24 fresh okra pods

1 cup almonds, roasted

1/2 onion

2 cloves garlic

1 (1-inch) piece fresh ginger

1 jalapeño, minced

1/2 teaspoon coriander

1/2 teaspoon salt

Directions

Preheat oven to 425 degrees F. Line a baking sheet with parchment paper.

Cut tops of okra. Split okra pods in halves lengthwise, and leave one side intact. Carefully pry pods open.

Bland almonds, onion, garlic, ginger, jalapeño, coriander, and salt in an electric blender or food processor.

Stuff okra pods with almond mixture. Place on prepared baking sheet and bake for 15 minutes, or until okra pods are tender. Serve immediately.

Spiced Cheese Poppers

(Ready in about 55 minutes | Servings 10)

Ingredients

1/3 cup all-purpose flour

1 large egg

1 teaspoon salt

2 tablespoons water

2/3 cup breadcrumbs

1 (11-ounce) soft chèvre

2 cups olive oil

1 tablespoon chives, minced

1/4 teaspoon paprika

Directions

Mix egg, 1/2 teaspoon salt, and 2 tablespoons water in a medium bowl. Mix breadcrumbs and remaining 1/2 teaspoon salt in another bowl.

Shape soft cheese into 24 balls. Coat cheese balls with flour, then dip in egg mixture, and finally coat with breadcrumb mixture. Freeze for 30 minutes.

Heat olive oil in a wide saucepan over medium flame. Fry prepared cheese balls until they are crisp.

Transfer fried cheese poppers on a serving tray. Sprinkle with chives and paprika and serve warm.

Stuffed Celery Fingers

(Ready in about 15 minutes | Servings 5)

Ingredients

3/4 cup Gouda, grated

2 ounces soft cheese

2 tablespoons mayonnaise

1/4 cup olives, pitted and chopped

2 red bell peppers, chopped

1/2 teaspoon onion powder

8 large ribs celery, cut into 1 1/2-inch lengths

2 tablespoons rosemary

Directions

To make the filling: Blend Gouda, soft cheese, mayonnaise, olives, peppers and onion powder.

Slice celery into 1 1/2-inch pieces lengthwise.

Carefully stuff celery pieces. Arrange on a serving platter, sprinkle with rosemary and serve.

Bruschetta with Eggplant and Feta

(Ready in about 45 minutes | Servings 4)

Ingredients

1 eggplant, cut into bite-sized cubes

1 onion, cut into rings

4 medium tomatoes, halved lengthwise, seeded, and slivered

4 tablespoons olive oil

1 teaspoon salt

1/4 teaspoon ground black pepper

4 slices bread

1/2 cup fresh mint leaves

1 tablespoon fresh lemon juice

4 ounces feta cheese, crumbled

Directions

Preheat oven to 450 degrees F. Oil a baking sheet.

Place eggplant, onion, tomatoes, and olive oil on the baking sheets. Season with salt and pepper and mix to combine. Roast until eggplant is soft, or for 30 minutes. Reserve.

Place bread on the baking sheet, and bake until golden.

Combine eggplant mixture with mint and lemon juice. Spread eggplant mixture on toasted bread slices, and then top with feta cheese.

Party Spiced Stuffed Eggs

(Ready in about 20 minutes | Servings 6)

Ingredients

- 6 hard-boiled egg
- 3 tablespoons mayonnaise
- 1 tablespoon balsamic vinegar
- 1 tablespoon lemon juice
- 1 small onion, finely chopped
- 1 jalapeño, minced
- 1 teaspoon salt
- 1/4 teaspoon black pepper
- 1/2 teaspoon red pepper flakes
- Cilantro for garnish
- Black olives for garnish (optional)

Directions

Gently slice eggs in halves, lengthwise.

To make the filling: Scoop out the yolks into a medium mixing bowl. Mash yolks by using a fork. Add mayonnaise and mix to combine.

Stir in vinegar and lemon juice. Add onion and jalapeño. Season with salt, black pepper and red pepper.

Stuff the eggs. Sprinkle cilantro, top with olives and transfer to a serving tray.

PART FIVE DESSERTS

Almond Summertime Treat

(Ready in about 3 hours 15 minutes | Servings 8)

Ingredients

1/4 cup almonds, blanched

2 cups milk

3/4 cup whipping heavy cream

3 egg yolks

1/2 cup fine white sugar

1 teaspoon brandy

Directions

Blend the almonds into a purée. Add milk and whipping cream, mix to combine all ingredients well. Bring the mixture to a boil.

In another bowl, mix egg yolks, sugar and brandy for 5 minutes. Stir in almond mixture and mix well.

Heat the mixture over low heat for 5 to 6 minutes, stirring frequently.

Let it cool. Freeze until the ice cream is completely frozen and firm.

Fruit-Nuts Ice Cream

(Ready in about 3 hours 15 minutes | Servings 10)

Ingredients

1 box frozen strawberries

1 cup hazelnuts

2 cans sweetened condensed milk

3 bananas, mashed

1 cup almonds

4 cups half-and-half

1 can pineapple, diced

Directions

Mix strawberries, hazelnuts, milk, mashed bananas, almonds, half-and-half and pineapple.

Put this mixture into an ice cream freeze. Freeze until the ice cream is firm and frozen.

Serve by using ice cream spoon and garnish with additional nuts.

Chocolate Maraschino Cakes

(Ready in about 1 hour | Servings 24)

Ingredients

2 tablespoons butter

1/2 cup sugar

1 square cooking chocolate

1 large egg

1 ¼ cups all-purpose flour

1/4 teaspoon baking soda

8 ounces cream cheese

1/2 cup sugar

1 large egg

24 maraschino cherry halves

Directions

Preheat oven to 350 degrees F. Butter a muffin tin.

Combine butter, sugar and melted cooking chocolate in a mixing bowl. Beat egg and add to the mixing bowl.

In another large bowl, combine flour and baking soda. Add to chocolate-egg mixture. Stretch a dough on lightly floured surface. Place the dough in the muffin tins.

To prepare the filling: Combine cream cheese, sugar and egg. Divide filling among cakes. Bake for 12 minutes.

Top prepared cakes with cherries and cool on a wire rack.

Cream Pudding Cake

(Ready in about 1 hour 45 minutes | Servings 12)

Ingredients

1/2 cup butter

1 cup water

1 cup pastry flour

4 eggs

8 ounces cream cheese

4 cups milk

3 (3-ounces) packages instant vanilla pudding mix

2 cups heavy cream

chocolate syrup for garnish

Directions

Preheat oven to 400 degrees F. Grease a baking pan.

To make a cake dough: Mix butter and water. Stir in flour and cook, stirring constantly. Gradually add eggs, one at a time, beating well.

Bake for 40 minutes. Allow to cool.

Combine together cream cheese and milk and mix until smooth. Add instant pudding and then add heavy cream. Drizzle chocolate syrup on top.

Chill cake before cutting and serving.

Grandma's Chocolate Pie

(Ready in about 35 minutes | Servings 8)

Ingredients

4 egg yolks

1 ¼ cups sugar

3 tablespoons cocoa

1 1/2 cups milk

For Meringue:
4 egg whites

8 tablespoons sugar

4 tablespoons all-purpose flour

1/2 stick butter

1/2 teaspoon cinnamon

unbaked pie crust

4 tablespoons cornstarch

Directions

Preheat oven to 350 degrees F.

Beat egg yolks. Blend sugar, cocoa, milk and flour. Combine with egg mixture.

Slice the butter into small pieces and add to the egg-flour mixture. Add cinnamon and mix to combine well.

Cook over medium-high heat until butter is melted. Pour cooked mixture into pie crust and bake about 30 minutes.

To make meringue: Beat egg whites. Mix in sugar with cornstarch. Beat for five minutes.

Spread meringue on the pie and bake for few minutes. Remove to a wire rack in order to cool.

Chocolate Sauce with Fresh Fruit

(Ready in about 40 minutes | Servings 6)

Ingredients

1 cup heavy cream

4 squares cooking chocolate

2 ½ superfine sugar

1/2 margarine

1/2 cup strong coffee

Fruits of choice

Directions

Place heavy cream, cooking chocolate, sugar, margarine and strong coffee in a double boiler.

Cook until the chocolate is melted.

Stir to combine all ingredients well.

Serve with your favorite fruits.

Caramels for Party Gifts

(Ready in about 45 minutes | Servings 64)

Ingredients

2 cups sugar

1 cup light cream

1 cup butter

1/2 cup corn syrup

4 unsweetened chocolate squares

1 ½ cups almonds, cut into halves

32 candied cherries

Directions

Preheat a wide cast-iron skillet over medium heat. Cook the sugar, light cream, butter, corn syrup and chocolate squares, stirring constantly to prevent burning. Bring to a gentle boil. Cook, until cooked mixture reaches 248 degrees on a candy thermometer.

Let it cool for 5 minutes. Add almonds.

Grease a square pan. Pour in the candy mixture. Cut candied cherries into halves. Cool candy mixture until it is firm.

Cut candy mixture into 64 caramels, so there is a cherry on each caramel.

Chocolate Cinnamon Loaf

(Ready in about 4 hours 30 minutes | Servings 16)

Ingredients

1/4 cup warm water

1 teaspoon honey

1 package yeast

1 cup milk

2 tablespoons butter

4 cups pastry flour

1/2 teaspoon cinnamon

1/4 teaspoon nutmeg

2/3 cup unsweetened cocoa powder

2 teaspoons instant coffee powder

1/2 cup sugar

2 eggs

1 cup hazelnuts, toasted and chopped

1/2 cup raisins

Directions

Combine the water and honey in a small bowl. Add the yeast and set aside for 10 minutes.

Heat the milk and butter in a deep saucepan to about 110 degrees.

Combine 3/4 cups flour, cinnamon, nutmeg, cocoa, coffee and the sugar. Mix well.

Beat eggs and add the warm milk-butter mixture. Combine this mixture along with yeast mixture and the flour. Stir in the hazelnuts and raisins. Mix all ingredients.

Transfer the dough onto floured surface and knead until the dough is elastic. Let rise in a warm place until dough is doubled.

Punch down the dough. Roll the dough and form into large round shape. Transfer the dough to a baking pan. Brush the dough with butter and let rise again about 1 hour.

Preheat oven to 350 degrees. Cover with a foil and bake chocolate loaf for 30 minutes, then uncover and bake for 25 minutes longer.

Let cool on a wire rack. Serve at room temperature.

Chocolate Squares with Nuts and Coconut

(Ready in about 15 minutes | Servings 16)

Ingredients

1/2 cup butter, softened

1 cup brown sugar

1 cup flour

2 large eggs

1 teaspoon vanilla extract

1 cup walnuts, chopped

1 cup coconut, flaked

1/2 teaspoon cinnamon

6 ounces chocolate chips

Directions

Blend butter and 1/2 cup of the sugar until smooth. Add the flour and combine well.

Place dough into an 8-inch square glass baking dish. Microwave on 100% power for 5 minutes.

Combine eggs, vanilla, walnuts, coconut, cinnamon, chocolate chips and remaining 1/2 sugar.

Spread egg-nuts mixture over baked crust. Microwave on 100% power for 5 minutes, or until set. Transfer on a wire rack and cool. After that slice into squares.

Carrot Cake with Almonds and Cheese Icing

(Ready in about 2 hours 30 minutes | Servings 16)

Ingredients

6 cups grated carrots

1 cup sugar

1 cup raisins

4 eggs

1 ½ cups superfine white sugar

1 cup canola oil

1 teaspoon vanilla extract

1 cup pineapple, drained

3 cups cake flour

1 teaspoon baking soda

3 teaspoons cinnamon

1 cup chopped almonds

½ cup (1 stick) butter, softened

1 teaspoon vanilla extract

8 ounces cream cheese, at room temperature

2½ cups powdered sugar

Directions

Combine together grated carrots and sugar. Set aside for 60 minutes. After that add raisins.

Preheat oven to 350 degrees F. Butter and flour two 10-inch cake pans.

Beat eggs and gradually add superfine white sugar, canola oil and vanilla. Chop the pineapple into very small chunks and add to egg mixture.

Combine the flour, baking soda, and cinnamon. Stir into the egg mixture. Stir in the carrot mixture and then add the almonds. Place the batter into prepared pans.

Bake about 50 minutes. Remove from the oven and allow to cool for a while.

To make the icing: Cream together the butter, vanilla, and cream cheese until smooth. Slowly add the powdered sugar and blend well to combine.

When the cake is completely cooled, spread the cream cheese icing all over the cake.

Pears with Chocolate Sauce

(Ready in about 40 minutes | Servings 6)

Ingredients

6 large fresh pears

5 cups white wine

1 cup sugar

3 teaspoons cinnamon

1 Vanilla bean

2 cinnamon sticks

1 cup heavy cream

4 squares baking chocolate

2 ½ cups powdered sugar

1/2 cup butter

1/2 cup strong coffee

Directions

Peel the pears and core from the bottom, leaving a 3/4-inch hole.

Add the wine, sugar, cinnamon and vanilla bean to a wide and deep saucepan. Bring to a boil and then add the pears. Cook until the pears are soft. Set aside.

To make a chocolate sauce: Place cream, baking chocolate, powdered sugar, butter, and strong coffee in a double boiler. Heat for 30 minutes. Mix well to combine all ingredients.

Ladle the chocolate sauce in a serving plate and place the pears.

Perfect Cake for the Evening

(Ready in about 50 minutes | Servings 16)

Ingredients

1 1/3 cups white sugar

2/3 cup butter

2 eggs

2 cups cake flour

2 teaspoons baking powder

2/3 cup milk

Icing sugar for garnish (optional)

Directions

Preheat oven to 350 degrees F. Grease and flour a 9x9 inch baking pan.

Mix together the sugar and butter. Beat the eggs, and stir in one at a time.

Sift the flour and baking powder, then add to the egg mixture. Stir well to combine all ingredients.

Stir in the milk and mix until batter is smooth. Pour batter into the baking pan.

Bake about 40 minutes, or until the cake springs back to the touch.

Dust with the icing sugar if desired. Serve at room temperature with a glass of warm milk.

Halloween Pumpkin Cheesecake

(Ready in about 4 hours + | Servings 8)

Ingredients

2 (8-ounce) packages cream cheese

1/2 cup superfine sugar

1/2 teaspoon vanilla extract

2 eggs

1 (9-inch) graham cracker crust

1/2 cup pumpkin purée

1/2 teaspoon cinnamon

1 pinch ground nutmeg

1/2 cup vanilla whipped topping

Directions

Preheat oven to 325 degrees F.

Combine cream cheese, sugar and vanilla, and mix well.

Beat in eggs one at a time. Take 1 cup of batter and set aside.

In the remaining batter, add pumpkin purée, cinnamon, and nutmeg. Mix until the mixture is blended. Layer blended mixture over the batter in the crust.

Bake for 35 to 40 minutes. Refrigerate overnight. Cover with whipped topping and serve chilled.

Creamy Dessert in a Glass

(Ready in about 10 minutes | Servings 1)

Ingredients

1 fluid ounce creme de cacao

1 fluid ounce Kahlua

1 fluid ounce white creme de menthe

1 fluid ounce sweet cream

Ice, cracked

Directions

Place cracked ice in a mixing glass. Add the creme de cacao, Kahlua, the creme de menthe, and sweet cream.

Shake and pour into a cocktail glass. Serve chilled.

Perfect Blackberry Ice Cream

(Ready in about 50 minutes + chilling | Servings 8)

Ingredients

4 cups fresh blackberries

1 cup water

1 cup white sugar

2 ½ cups whipping cream

fresh mint leaves for garnish

Directions

Line a colander with two layers of wetted cheesecloth. Place over a wide bowl.

To make the blackberry juice: Mix blackberries and water in a deep saucepan. Bring to a boil over medium heat and then lower the heat and simmer for 10 to 12 minutes. Pour into cheesecloth-lined strainer. Allow to stand for at least 30 minutes.

To make the syrup: Pour blackberry juice into another saucepan. Stir in the sugar and cook over low heat for 10 minutes. Let it cool completely.

Combine syrup with whipping cream. Transfer to a refrigerator.

Blend blackberry cream in ice cream maker according to manufacturer's instructions. Freeze for several hours. Garnish with mint leaves and serve chilled.

Pecan Vanilla Ice Cream

(Ready in about 15 minutes + chilling | Servings 8)

Ingredients

1 cup pecans

3 tablespoons butter, melted

4 eggs

2 ½ cups sugar

1 can condensed milk

1 small package vanilla instant pudding

1 tablespoon vanilla extract

Directions

Melt and heat the butter and sauté pecans until golden. Let it cool.

Beat eggs, gradually add sugar, and mix well to combine. Stir in canned milk and instant pudding. Add vanilla extract and prepared pecans.

Use freezer according to manufacturer's instructions.

Mom's Butter Cake

(Ready in about 50 minutes | Servings 6)

Ingredients

1 ¼ cups cake flour

1 ¾ cups light brown sugar

1/2 cup cocoa powder

2 teaspoons baking powder

2/3 cup milk

1 tablespoon lemon zest

2 tablespoons butter, melted

2 cups hot water

Directions

Preheat the oven to 350 degrees F.

Sift the flour, and combine with 3/4 cup of the brown sugar, 1/4 cup of the cocoa and baking powder. Add the milk, melted butter, and lemon zest and mix until well blended.

Spread prepared batter evenly into a baking pan.

Mix the remaining 1/4 cup of cocoa and 1 cup of brown sugar. Layer evenly over the prepared batter. Gently pour on the hot water.

Bake for 35 minutes and serve.

The Best Gingerbread Ever

(Ready in about 1 hour | Servings 10)

Ingredients

1/2 cup butter

1 ¼ cup honey

1 cup water

1/2 cup brown sugar

1 egg

1¾ cups unbleached white flour

2 teaspoons baking soda

1 tablespoon ground ginger

2 teaspoons ground cinnamon

1 teaspoon nutmeg, grated

2 teaspoons minced fresh ginger

Confectioners' sugar

Directions

Preheat the oven to 350 degrees F. Grease 8 x 8-inch square baking pan and set aside.

Combine the butter, honey, and water in a wide and deep saucepan. Cook until the butter begins to melt, stir often. Reserve.

In a small bowl, beat the sugar and egg.

In another mixing bowl, combine together flour, baking soda, ground ginger, cinnamon, nutmeg and fresh ginger. Mix well to combine all ingredients. Stir in the butter-honey mixture and the egg mixture. Mix again.

Pour the batter into the prepared baking pan. Bake for 30 to 40 minutes.

Remove the cake from the oven and let it cool on a wire rack.

Dust with confectioners' sugar and serve warm or at room temperature.

Peach and Almond Cake

(Ready in about 1 hour 10 minutes | Servings 9)

Ingredients

1/2 cup margarine, softened

1 cup sugar

1/2 cup almonds, finely chopped

1/2 cup all-purpose flour

1 teaspoon baking powder

2 eggs

1/2 teaspoon almond extract

4 ripe peaches, peeled

1 tablespoon butter

1 tablespoon sugar

2 tablespoons all-purpose flour

1/2 teaspoon cinnamon

Directions

Preheat the oven to 350 degrees F. Grease a baking pan (9-inch size).

To make the batter: Combine the margarine and sugar and mix until blended. Add the almonds, flour, baking powder, eggs, and almond extract, and beat until the mixture is very fluffy.

Spread the batter into the baking pan. Slice the peaches and place on the cake in one layer.

To make the topping: Mix together the butter, sugar, flour, and cinnamon. Mix until it is the texture of coarse crumbs. Sprinkle on the top of the cake.

Bake for 50 to 60 minutes. Cool on a wire rack for 10 minutes and serve at room temperature.

Holiday Fruit Tart

(Ready in about 40 minutes + chilling | Servings 8)

Ingredients

14 graham cracker halves

1/4 cup butter, melted

2 tablespoons sugar

1/4 teaspoon cinnamon

8 ounces cream cheese

1/4 cup honey

1 teaspoon vanilla extract

2 ripe apricots, peeled

3 ripe peaches, peeled

2/3 cup raspberries

2 tablespoons raspberry jelly

1/2 teaspoon water

Directions

Preheat the oven to 350 degrees F. Butter a pie plate.

To prepare the crust: Put the graham crackers in a plastic bag and crush it with a rolling pin.

Transfer crushed crackers in a bowl, and combine the butter, sugar, and cinnamon. Mix well to combine. Place prepared mixture in the pie plate and bake for 10 minutes. Reserve.

To prepare the filling: Mix together cream cheese, honey, and vanilla until smooth. Spread evenly onto the bottom of the pie shell.

To make the topping: Slice apricots and peaches into thin slices and place around the edge of the tart. Use the raspberries to make a border around the outer edge of the tart.

To make the glaze: Heat raspberry jelly and water, until it is smooth. Spread all the glaze onto the tart. Chill the prepared fruit tart for 2 hours.

Apple Crisp with Ice Cream

(Ready in about 45 minutes | Servings 6)

Ingredients

8 apples, peeled, cored, and thinly sliced

1/4 cup water

3 tablespoons firmly packed brown sugar

1/2 teaspoon cinnamon

1 teaspoon vanilla extract

1/2 cup pastry flour

1/2 cup firmly packed brown sugar

1 teaspoon cinnamon

6 tablespoons butter

almond ice cream (optional)

Directions

Preheat the oven to 350 degrees F.

Place the slices of the apples in an ovenproof dish. Pour the water over them, then sprinkle the sugar, cinnamon and vanilla extract and toss carefully.

To prepare the topping: Combine the flour, sugar, and cinnamon in a mixing bowl, and mix well to combine ingredients.

Cut the butter into the mixture. Spread evenly over the apples.

Bake for 30 to 40 minutes, or until the apples are very soft and golden. Allow to cool for a while. Top with ice cream and serve at room temperature.

Stuffed Peaches on Almond-Flavored Whipped Cream

(Ready in about 20 minutes | Servings 4)

Ingredients

1 cup fresh dark cherries, pitted and sliced

1/3 cup almonds, finely chopped

3 teaspoons superfine sugar

4 ripe peaches

juice form 1 lemon

2/3 cup whipping cream

1½ tablespoons powdered sugar

1/2 teaspoon almond extract

Directions

To make the filling: Combine the cherries, almonds, and sugar in a mixing bowl.

Peel the peaches and slice them in half. Remove the stones, and scoop out a little of the center of a flesh.

Pour the lemon juice in a deep dish and place peaches in it, in order to prevent discoloration.

Fill the peach halves with the cherry filling. Place the stuffed peaches in a shallow dish.

To make the almond-flavored cream: Beat the whipping cream in a mixing bowl for 4 to 5 minutes. Then add the powdered sugar and almond extract. Continue to beat for a few minutes more.

Divide the cream among serving bowls. Place stuffed peach halves on a bed of almond-flavored whipped cream.

Peanut Butter Oatmeal Cookies

(Ready in about 30 minutes | Servings 12)

Ingredients

1½ cups unbleached flour

½ cup rolled oats

½ teaspoon baking soda

1/2 teaspoon salt

1 cup brown sugar

1/4 cup vegetable shortening

1/4 cup grape seed oil

1/4 cup peanut butter, softened

1 tablespoon egg replacer powder

1 teaspoon vanilla extract

1 cup chocolate chips

Directions

Preheat oven to 375 degrees F. Line a cookie sheet with a parchment paper.

Combine flour, oats, baking soda and salt and mix well.

Mix sugar, shortening, oil and butter in another bowl with an electric mixer until smooth.

Combine 5 tablespoons water, egg replacer powder and vanilla. Add this mixture to sugar mixture and mix well to combine.

Combine together dry mixture and wet mixture and add chocolate chips.
Shape the batter into small balls, then press the cookies to flatten.

Transfer the cookies to prepared cookie sheet and bake for 12 minutes until the cookies are crisp and golden. Allow to cool before serving.

Pears with Almond Topping

(Ready in about 1 hour | Servings 6)

Ingredients

3 eggs

1/4 cup honey

1 ¼ teaspoon almond extract

1/4 teaspoon nutmeg, grated

1/4 teaspoon cardamom

1½ cups milk

1/3 cup flour

4 ripe pears, peeled and cored

1/2 cup Crisp Topping, made with almonds

Directions

Preheat the oven to 375 degrees F. Grease a pie plate.

Place the eggs, honey, almond extracts, nutmeg, cardamom, milk, and flour in a blender and mix until smooth. Reserve until ready to use.

Cut the pears into thin slices and layer them onto the prepared pie plate. Pour the batter over the pears, and top with Crisp Topping.

Bake for about 50 minutes. Let it cool for a few minutes and serve.

Frozen Honey and Pistachios Mousse

(Ready in about 20 minutes + chilling | Servings 8)

Ingredients

1 cup whipping cream

3 egg yolks

1/2 cup honey

2 tablespoons orange zest

1/4 cup pistachios, peeled and chopped

1 tablespoon orange flower water

Directions

Whip the cream until it holds soft. Let it cool in a refrigerator.

Blend the yolks and honey until they thicken. Add the zest, pistachios, and orange water. Blend until all ingredients are well combined.

Freeze for 3 hours before serving.

Lemon Oat Cake

(Ready in about 45 minutes | Servings 10)

Ingredients

3/4 cup rolled oats

3/4 cup pastry flour

1/4 cup almond flour

1/4 cup maple syrup

1/4 cup coconut oil, melted

4 eggs

2 egg yolks

1/2 cup lemon juice

3/4 cup sugar

1/3 cup almond flour

Icing sugar, for dusting

Directions

Preheat the oven to 350 degrees F. Butter an 8 x 8-inch baking pan.

To make the crust: Mix the oats and flours on medium-high for 20 seconds. Add maple syrup and coconut oil, and blend for 20 seconds.

Transfer to the baking pan and bake for 15 minutes.

To make the filling: Place whole eggs, egg yolks, lemon juice, sugar and almond flour and blend until the mixture is frothy.

Pour the mixture over the crust and bake for 25 minutes more. Dust with icing sugar and serve.

Chocolate Avocado Mousse

(Ready in about 25 minutes + chilling | Servings 6)

Ingredients

5 dates, pitted

1/2 cup hot water

1/4 cup chocolate chips

1/4 cup milk

2 ripe avocados, peeled

1/2 cup unsweetened cocoa powder

2 tablespoons honey

1 teaspoon instant coffee

1 tablespoon almond extract

Directions

Place the dates in a deep bowl and cover with water. Let soak for 15 minutes.

Melt the chocolate chips in a double boiler. Reserve.

Drain the dates and put them in the blender. Pulse several times.

Pour in the milk, and then add avocados, cocoa powder, honey, instant coffee, almond extract, and chilled chocolate. Blend until the mixture is smooth.

Transfer the mixture into 4-ounce ramekins. Chill for at least 3 hours.

Cardamom Butter Cookies

(Ready in about 25 minutes | Servings 10)

Ingredients

1/2 cup unsalted butter, softened

1/2 cup powdered sugar

2 tablespoons granulated sugar

1 egg yolk

1 teaspoon ground cardamom

1/4 teaspoon cinnamon

1/4 teaspoon salt

1¼ cups all-purpose flour

Directions

Cream the butter, powdered and granulated sugar until everything is combined well. Beat in the egg yolk. Stir in the cardamom, cinnamon, salt, and flour.

Divide the dough in two, roughly shape pieces, and then roll in plastic wrap. Let rest in a refrigerator.

Preheat the oven to 375 degrees F. Cut dough into as many rounds as possible and place them on a baking pan. Bake for 8 to 10 minutes. Let it cool. Dust with confectioners' sugar and serve.

Teatime Sandwich Cookies

(Ready in about 1 hour | Servings 18)

Ingredients

1¼ cups all-purpose flour

1 cup sugar

1/2 cup unsweetened cocoa powder

1/4 teaspoon salt

1/4 teaspoon baking powder

1/2 cup margarine

3 tablespoons milk

1 teaspoon pure vanilla extract

1/4 cup non-hydrogenated vegetable shortening

1/4 cup margarine

2 cups powdered sugar

1 teaspoon pure vanilla extract

Directions

In a food processor, blend flour, sugar, cocoa, salt, and baking powder until everything is well combined. Add margarine, milk, and vanilla extract and pulse a few more times.

Transfer the batter to a large bowl and knead several times. Let rest in a refrigerator.

Preheat the oven to 350 degrees F. Line 2 baking sheets with parchment paper.

Roll a heaping teaspoon of dough into a ball. Place the batter onto prepared baking sheets. Flatten the dough and bake for 14 minutes.

To make the filling: Mix the shortening and margarine until smooth. Add powdered sugar and vanilla extract, and mix until all ingredients are well blended. Beat for 2 more minutes.

To assemble the cookies: Spread a filling on the flat bottom side of the cookies. Place the flat bottom side of another cookie on top. Gently press the cookies together.

Arrange to a serving tray.

Peanut Butter Cookies

(Ready in about 40 minutes | Servings 12)

Ingredients

1¼ cups all-purpose flour

1 teaspoon baking soda

1/4 teaspoon salt

1/2 cup peanut butter

1/2 cup butter

1 cup sugar

2 teaspoons vanilla extract

1 tablespoon water

Directions

Preheat the oven to 350 degrees F. Line 3 baking sheets with Silpat.

In a mixing bowl, combine together flour, baking soda, and salt. Reserve.

Using a mixer, beat peanut butter, butter, sugar, vanilla, and water until the mixture is fluffy.

Stir in the flour mixture. Scoop 2 tablespoons of dough at a time onto the prepared baking sheets. Using back of a fork, lightly press the dough.

Bake for 12 minutes, or until the edges of the cookies are lightly browned. Let cool on a wire rack.

Download a FREE PDF file with photos of all the recipes by following the link:

Made in the USA
Monee, IL
17 December 2019